Male Sex Work in the Digital Age

Paul Ryan

Male Sex Work in the Digital Age

Curated Lives

palgrave
macmillan

Paul Ryan
Maynooth University
Maynooth, Ireland

ISBN 978-3-030-11796-2   ISBN 978-3-030-11797-9   (eBook)
https://doi.org/10.1007/978-3-030-11797-9

Library of Congress Control Number: 2018968341

This Palgrave Macmillan imprint is published by the registered company Springer Nature Switzerland AG
The registered company address is: Gewerbestrasse 11, 6330 Cham, Switzerland

Acknowledgements

I was fortunate to receive assistance and support from many people during the completion of this book. I want to thank all the men who trusted me with their stories included in this book, particularly at a time when sex workers remain subject to stigma and criminalisation. Thanks to Amelia Derkatsch at Palgrave. Thanks to Sex Workers Alliance Ireland for their support and my colleagues from COST Action IS1209 'Comparing European Prostitution Policies: Understanding Scales and Cultures of Governance' 2013–2017. Thanks to my colleagues in the Department of Sociology and the Maynooth University Social Sciences Institute (MUSSI). Special thanks to my family and friends. This book is dedicated to my brother, Dermot Ryan, and is in memory of Laura Lee (1979–2018).

Contents

1

The Changing World of Online Male Sex Work

Abstract In this introductory chapter Ryan sets out five developments that have had a direct impact on the growing importance of new social media in understanding transformations within male sex work. These are (1) the normalization of the sex industry (2) the rise of new social media (3) micro-celebrity and self-branding (4) fetishising and racialising muscular bodies in erotic labour, and (5) the gig economy. The chapter concludes with a discussion of the historical and political context of sex work in Ireland and abroad.

Keywords Sex industry · Celebrity · Bodies · Gig economy · Male sex work

Introduction

I was waiting for an appearance on a current affairs television programme, when the host, Vincent Browne, came to greet me. After the briefest of pleasantries, Browne told me that he thought that men who bought sex from women were clearly pathological. This was, 'not

© The Author(s) 2019   **1**
P. Ryan, *Male Sex Work in the Digital Age*,
https://doi.org/10.1007/978-3-030-11797-9_1

in dispute' I was told. It was an ominous start. I had been asked on the programme to discuss a proposal put forward by a parliamentary sub-committee that would criminalise the purchase of sex. However, a discussion of the proposal did not happen. The debate, with the chief executive of an organisation that supports the exit of women from prostitution,[1] settled into a familiar routine. I spoke of the complexity within sex work and the absence of any carceral, magic bullet solution that could address the structural inequalities of those lives. I was told, in line with a neo-abolitionist approach to prostitution (Barry 1995; O'Connor and Healy 2006), that trafficking and violence were indistinguishable from sex work. Consent was deemed irrelevant, men who buy sex were pathological and those that sold sex were statistically irrelevant.

Men who sell sex are not irrelevant though. I had interviewed male sex workers since 2009, and there was an existing body of research that had explored their experiences for over twenty years. I knew the circumstances of their consent were important and that their removal from public debate, while convenient politics, may have a detrimental outcome on the targeted provision of services that addressed their health and safety. Male or trans sex workers represented 9% of all commercial sex transactions in Ireland (Maginn and Ellison 2014). The research I undertook for this book suggested that the impact of migration and the use of new digital cultures had transformed male sex work. My interviews with eighteen Brazilian and Venezuelan men engaged in commercial sex while living in Dublin revealed the extent of that transformation, through innovative ways in which they have harnessed their micro-celebrity on new social media to broadcast monetised content on video sharing platforms. These men curate different digital selves that are tailored for specific audiences on apps like Grindr, Instagram, Twitter and Tinder. In this book, I concentrate on Grindr and Instagram. Both offer an insight into two digital lives; one transitory and opportunistic (Grindr), the other a more intimate and permanent biography (Instagram). Their involvement in sex work remains ambiguous across both platforms. My interviewees speak about what they *do*, not about who they *are*. They are not sex work rights activists. However, they also seek no rescue, redemption or exit promised by NGOs committed to the abolition of prostitution. Some men strongly dislike sex work. Others are actively shaping a range of online sex work practices that best suit the circumstances of their lives. There are no happy hooker tropes here. They are charting a way through the discourses of coercion and rights. They are reluctant to advertise sexual services on exclusively escort sites, like rentboy.com and later rentmen. eu.[2] Rather their potential clients read and decipher photos, emoji and text on Grindr or join thousands of other followers on Instagram, where they are invited to interact and proceed to access monetised content or arrange face-to-face meetings.[3] It was clear from the outset of this book that the lived realities and experiences of men in sex work bore little resemblance to the legal and political discourses that framed the debate.

Five developments have encouraged the movement of male sex work further within the digital cultures of new social media. These are important to understand the structure and stories within this book.

1. *The Normalisation of the Sex Industry*
This study was undertaken within a context of the ongoing normalisation of the sex industry. This development has a number of facets. There has been a documented increased visibility of adult entertainment industries throughout cities in Europe, driven by local governance laws and sex-related tourism (Hubbard et al. 2008: 376). This tourism, combined with a growth in the leisure industry, technology and changing consumer patterns has contributed to this increased visibility of sexual commerce, blurring the boundaries between mainstream industries (Brents and Sanders 2010: 376; Sanders et al. 2018: 2). This normalisation is particularly evident in relation to male sex work. Later in this chapter, I discuss how the social meanings attached to male prostitution have changed over history, where it was the association with homosexuality and class transgression that located the practice within a deviancy perspective (MacPhail et al. 2015: 485). The aspirations of the post decriminalisation gay movement were forged under unique economic circumstances that saw Ireland emerge as the clearest example of small country liberalism in Europe (Ó Riain 2014: 9). Pro-market reforms combined with a leaner government and a 'privatized economy' could now coexist with a politics of identity and equality. In Ireland and other liberal

economies, issue of care and social reproduction continued to be privatised or to be deemed the personal responsibility of families or wider civil society. Under such a framework, I argue that liberalism needed to 'create' new families to share the burden of this redistribution of social costs leading to broad political support for gay marriage, successfully passed by referendum in 2015. Male sex work has been a beneficiary of this legislative success, where men have been afforded greater agency and respectability for their sexual entrepreneurship, in sharp contrast to the exclusively coercive portrayal of female workers. Male sex work has benefited from the technological revolution that has dramatically reduced the existence of street work, increasing the number of middle-class workers attracted by greater privacy, safety and flexibility from working at home (McLean 2013). In Chapter 3, I argue that it is within this technology, like the dating app Grindr that male sex work has become the most visible, blurring boundaries between economic and physical capital in sex, dating and relationships. In this reimagining of intimate relationships, distinguishing between those who possess agency and power with coercion and victimhood becomes a more nuanced endeavour.

2. *The Rise of New Social Media Applications*

New social media has become an important site where individuals construct, reimagine and perform identities to audiences in late modern societies. While previously associated with social networking sites like Facebook, where the impetus was to connect to other users (Van Dijck 2013), a visual turn in society and social media specifically, has created platforms less about sharing content, and more about performing identities through consumption (Walsh and Baker 2017). Social media users communicate taste, cultural capital and self-discipline through their consumption to an increasingly diverse group of followers that is maintained and grown through the judicious use of hashtags (Page 2012). Instagram, the photo and video sharing app founded in 2010 is leading the way in this visual turn, reporting 1 billion monthly users in 2018.[4] I argue that material, especially self-photography or selfies, uploaded on Instagram and Grindr are the raw material of digital identities and have become an exchange currency of both the validation and domination of others who fail to meet benchmarks of popularity, fitness, travel or friendship. They become a currency that can be traded and converted. It is a currency that can open new economic opportunities as the self itself becomes a commodity for online advertising. Social media followers are directed to Instagram through the use of hashtags and links from apps like Grindr. In Chapter 4, I argue that this facilitates a new dimension of intimacy within the client-sex worker relationship, not present in traditional escort websites, by granting followers access into the men's everyday lives. It also transforms our understanding of the online world, which ceases to be a mere storage depot for data, photos and chat (Batty 1997) becoming a gateway that places the material body as central to online interaction. Potential clients of male sex workers can avail of a real-time and highly choreographed experience facilitated by the frequent use of features like Instagram Story that allows men to post short videos of their daily lives.

Grindr, founded in 2009, for men who seek sex with men is a mobile app with global positioning technology that facilitates the interaction and trade of messages and photos (Brennan 2017). In Chapter 3, I argue that male sex workers are using their personal profiles to market sexual services. I argue that male sex workers thrive on Grindr where the digital visibility and fetishisation of the muscular body bestows a physical and erotic capital. If Instagram provided a platform for the construction of a digital narrative that was consistent, Grindr provided the direct opposite. The digital self on Grindr was transient, where men alternated photos sometimes on daily basis that ranged between shirtless changing room selfies, holiday beach photos or occasionally, a blank black screen. The ease with which photos and emoji were changed, constantly communicating different messages to different audiences facilitated the rise of the opportunistic, pop-escort. Grindr opened new hybrid spaces that lie between the digital and the physical that, when facilitated by mobile technology, can reshape space in ways that are transformative and transgressive (Ryan 2016; Kitchin and Dodge 2011; De Souza e Silva 2006). It allowed sex workers to navigate the city—in either Dublin or Dubai—creating new opportunities in diverse physical locations like bars, clubs, gyms, airports or places of worship. The stories in this book reveal that while this transience brought great freedom to recreate and tailor the self to diverse audiences, trading exclusively on the digital visibility of their physical and erotic capital brought with it the unintended consequence of coercive situations and emotional distress.

3. *Micro-Celebrity and Self-Branding*

Self-branding is a form of labour undertaken in late modern, or post-Fordist economies. I understand it in the context of Giddens' (1991: 5) reflexive project of the self where the individual must take it upon themselves to access resources and choose lifestyle options that are necessary to engage in an active, ongoing construction of their biographical narrative. This concept of lifestyle gives 'material form' to self-identity and becomes expressed as set of practices or routines most often incorporated into patterns of consumption with habits governing modes of dress, food and behaviour (p. 113). The body plays a key role within this reflexive project becoming a visible means of transmitting identity through the physique (Giddens 1992: 31). In Chapter 2, I return to these themes, drawing from Bourdieu (1986) to explore this embodied dimension of cultural capital that conveys status and power. Using interview data, I argue how the male sex worker body bears the imprint of social class and communicates habitus and economic location to social media followers and in real-time locations like the gym.

With the proliferation of new social media, self-branding has adopted a distinctive character. A new lexicon has emerged to describe how individuals construct and manage high-profile public identities on social media to gain either commercial opportunities and/or accrue cultural capital (Khamis et al. 2017); 'influencers' and the 'instafamous' deploy micro-celebrity (Senft 2008) interactive techniques to create an illusion of intimacy and trust between them and their followers. Such direct access to tens of thousands of largely younger consumers combined with an emotional connection that fosters trust and authenticity is hugely attractive to advertisers keen to harness the consumer reach of those bestowed with 'Instafame' (Marwick 2015). The political economy of Instafame rests securely on neoliberal foundations that commodifies the self, turning it into a brand that requires strategic cultivation and promotion to realise its full potential. Like any brand, injudicious social media posts that call into question the creditability and authenticity of the micro-celebrity can damage the commoditised self.

In Chapter 4, I use the concepts of Instafame (Marwick 2015), celebrity (Van Krieken 2012; Rojek 2001) and micro-celebrity (Senft 2008; Marwick 2013) as mechanisms to understand the social media use of a number of my interviewees. I explore how these men, with tens of thousands of followers construct their social media profiles broadcasting content that speaks to different audiences and how they navigate the self-branding of their bodies and lifestyles while maintaining an ambiguity about their sex work. I illustrate how technological developments like Instagram Story, live streaming, direct messaging and the polling of followers all foster micro-celebrity interaction. These technologies act as gatekeepers, allowing my interviewees to manage interaction, guiding followers through the promise of greater intimate access by purchasing content. My interviewees' use of Instagram works in tandem with other digital platforms like the gift registry site Amazon Wish List and OnlyFans, a site that encourages social media personalities to broadcast content on a subscription basis to their followers. My interviewees' use of OnlyFans reveals the competition of digital self-branding as broadcasters vie with each other to create and promote personalised and niche content to their audiences.

4. *Fetishising and Racialising Muscular Bodies in Erotic Labour*
Late modern societies have placed the body at the centre of a reflexive project of the self (Giddens 1991; Bauman 2000; Featherstone 2010). The body becomes a project that requires constant maintenance and alteration, where its value derives more from what it *looks* like rather than what it can *do*, in a context where the physical capabilities of the body in the labour force have been greatly diminished in advanced industrial society. The body becomes a bearer of symbolic value carrying the imprint of social class in how it is maintained, treated and shaped (Bourdieu 1986). It also communicates neoliberal ethics of individual responsibility showcasing the discipline, which has been imposed upon it through diet and exercise.

This has coincided with an increased gaze on the male body across advertising, film and popular culture within wider society (Patterson and Elliott 2002). Within urban gay culture, this fetishisation of the white, muscular male body although not new, is accelerated by the digital exchange of the body across new social media. This has greatly increased the value of the physical and erotic capital derived from this fetishised body.

In Chapter 3, I explore my interviewees' participation in a range of body projects, often originating in sport and fitness on the beaches of Brazil and Venezuela and now relocated within Dublin city centre gyms. I argue these men recognised early the physical capital with which their bodies possessed and the ability to deploy them to capitalise on economic and social opportunities within the world of dating, education and work. As newly arrived migrants, my interviewees faced challenges navigating high apartment rental prices often combined with minimum wage employment while struggling to repay debts accumulated in their relocation to Ireland. Grindr facilitated the display and conversion of this physical and erotic capital, drawn upon as a resource to meet financial needs and to support travel, social activities and consumer purchases.

The racialisation of desire played an important role in my interviewees' success in the digital sex and dating marketplace. In Chapters 2 and 3, I discuss how this became a double-edged sword. This process of racialisation of their erotic labour was happening within the context of widespread racism on Grindr profiles communicated through a language of 'personal preference' that excluded ethnic minorities (e.g. Daroya 2018). We know that racial hierarchies exist within sex work (Mahdavi 2010: 946; Jones 2015: 790). Technology is also complicit, with profiles constructed drawing from a drop-down list of ethnicities while in-app filters allow users to remove profile results that do not match their search parameters, most often excluding Asian men or large or stocky body types (Robinson 2015: 319). Although identified as Latino, my interviewees were born in countries with a rich history of migration and as such reflected that ethnic diversity, posing a challenge for them navigating clients that wanted an imagined exotic other—brown-eyed that was not too pale, but not too dark. Research on racialised gay sexualities online found that participants categorised Latinos as sensual, exotic and passionate (Paul et al. 2010), creating parameters with which sex workers constructed their racial identities online.

5. *The Gig Economy*

Ireland's open economy, heavily dependent on foreign direct investment in technology, pharmaceuticals and medical devices has suffered a roller-coaster ride of economic boom and bust, intensified by the global recession 2007–2012. It is now staging a dramatic recovery, recording a growth rate of 5.6%, predicted to be the highest in the European Union in 2018.[5] Various accounts of these tumultuous economic events have been told (e.g. Ó Riain 2014; Allen 2000). The economic consequences of that recession on the labour market remain. The effect of fiscal austerity, unemployment and rising labour precarity set the stage for an intensification of the on-demand or gig economy (Van Doorn 2017: 900). Digital connectivity has seen the rise of labour platforms where workers and clients can post jobs, rates per hour and work availability. The gig economy has been heralded for enabling workers to transcend the limitations of local labour markets and tap into international opportunities, allowing migrants circumvent local labour restrictions (Graham et al. 2017: 138, 147). However, digital labour does reduce bargaining power and increase precarity, particularly given its racialised and gendered characteristics. This results in a renegotiation of the social contract with workers where they assume all the risks and responsibilities of their labour (Van Doorn 2017: 902, 906).

Workers in the sex industry are familiar with precarious labour conditions. The status of the industry has left workers in most jurisdictions outside the protections of labour law (Berg and Penley 2016: 163). The stories in this book are located within the digital gig economy and illustrate how migrant workers, restricted under their visa conditions from working more than 20 hours per week, developed social media profiles that enabled them to broadcast monetised content and cultivate relationships with regular sex work clients. They also had previously worked on helpling.com, an online cleaning platform. These stories reveal how my interviewees remained wary of becoming reliant on their exclusively digital work on OnlyFans and jettisoning relationships with real-time clients. This digital work did however recalibrate the balance between their different sources of income as waiters, sex workers and online broadcasters of content. The stories in this book were told in specific cultural and historical moments of time. I want to next outline both the changing meaning of male prostitution and establish the social and political context of sex work in Ireland.

Changing Social Meanings of Male Sex Work

The meanings and motivations of those involved in male prostitution continued to evolve in tandem with the emergence of the homosexual as a scientific category in the late nineteenth century. Male prostitution became institutionalised in most European cities by the end of the seventeenth century, complete with spaces and language to facilitate it (Logan 2017: 22). The rise of sexology brought a scientific lens to understanding anomalies between the newly 'discovered' category of the homosexual and male prostitutes who identified as heterosexual. As this homosexual identity and personhood emerged, it became increasingly difficult for these participants—both buyers and sellers of sex—to remain immune from the new meanings that were associated with sexual acts previously thought of as mere transgressions of normative sexuality. These new meanings did not however equally apply across society. New classifications, typologies and binaries did not gain traction in urban working-class communities until the 1930s and 1940s, where a belief persisted that 'inverts' or effeminates represented the true homosexuality, as opposed to the more traditionally gendered 'perverts' (Kaye 2003: 3–4; Chauncey 1994: 14–15). Chauncey argues that sexually active men had a gendered identity rather than a sexual identity at the turn of the century, allowing for a distinction between conventional 'masculine' men and effeminate others known as pansies or fairies (1994: 48). How the legal or medical professions would treat or sanction those categories would similarly follow class lines, with the middle-class 'invert' subjected to greater leniency than the 'perversion' of their working-class counterpart. Many men adopted female personas through dress, make-up and mannerism to advertise their availability for sex with homosexual and straight men—with some crossing between effeminate and straight worlds depending on the safety of the locale (1994: 51). Fairies, like female prostitutes, had considerable success in attracting clients by offering oral sex; a service many 'respectable' women would not conduct, simultaneously making them objects of desire, tolerance and abuse. Middle- or upper-class fairies that offered local youth money for sex often became the victims of assault and theft as men sought to reinforce a traditional masculine dominance through violence or sexual brutalism (1994: 60). The word fairy would increasingly become used to identify effeminate men who sold sex to 'normal' men frequenting bars on the lower East side but also in brothels (1994: 67–68) where services were often easier and cheaper to locate than in female prostitution. The rise of greater gay visibility would restrict the numbers of men who identified as heterosexual from engaging in male prostitution, leading gay identified men to sell sex to each other for the first time (Kaye 2003: 37).

The Cleveland Street and Dublin Castle Scandals

The intersection between male prostitution and class created fears within British society about the impact of sexual degeneracy on the continued dominance of the Empire. The private sexual lives of individuals would become a microcosm of a wider moral panic at the heart of the nation and the masculinities within them. The Cleveland Street scandal in 1889–1890 fuelled a perception of sexually debauched elites largely immune from criminal sanction. The arrest and questioning of a fifteen-year-old boy on suspicious of theft led to an investigation that uncovered that he was one of a number of telegraph messenger boys employed by the General Post Office who worked in a homosexual brothel at 19 Cleveland Street in London's Fitzroy Square. The work of telegraph boys placed them in a unique position to cross not just the urban landscape but also cross class divides as they entered rarefied aristocratic circles to deliver correspondence at any time, day or night without causing suspicion (Hindmarch-Watson 2012: 599). An investigation commissioned by the GPO in 1877 into homosexuality and male prostitution amongst telegraph boys had identified boys from the poorest areas of Victorian London as being most likely to be associated with such behaviour, while lamenting being unable to hire a 'superior class' of boy for the meagre wages offered (p. 607). The report recommended that GPO officials inspect the homes of prospective telegraph boys to assess their living conditions, and moral character was part of a wider system of Victorian surveillance targeted at the poor. Although the report confirms that some boys had been dismissed from their jobs, there is evidence of a policy of containment. The investigation had led to just one prosecution of a worker deemed to have corrupted the younger boys, illustrating little desire to proceed with criminal charges, although this was a more difficult task before the passing of the Criminal Law Amendment Act in 1885.[6]

In Ireland, the General Post Office was also the centre of sexual intrigue and controversy involving male prostitution when a scandal involving high-level members of the English administration in Dublin Castle was made public. An article published in *United Ireland*[7] newspaper in 1883 suggested the Crown restrict 'the life and adventures' of various employees mentioning specifically James Ellis French, the Director of Detectives for Dublin Castle. French responded with a libel suit against William O'Brien, the editor of *United Ireland*, who in turn launched a private investigation into the alleged behaviour uncovering further evidence against other English bureaucrats—in particular Gustavus Cornwall, Irish Secretary to the General Post Office. After libel cases by French, and later Cornwall failed, the men along with six others were arrested on charges of sodomy. While Cornwall and a fellow accused, Martin Kirwin, a captain in the Royal Dublin Fusiliers, was acquitted, French was found guilty and sentenced to two years imprisonment.

The Dublin Castle Scandal associated key elements of the English administration in Ireland with male prostitution providing cultural and political nationalism with an opportunity to simultaneously assert the moral distinctiveness of Gaelic Ireland while illustrating the corruption and immorality that lay at the heart of colonial rule. It facilitated the construction of a despised colonial 'other' where homosexuality would define the very boundaries of the imagined Irish nation and that of its citizenship. 'Sexual respectability' would be crucial in defining the nation state (Mosse 1985: 1). The British administration would lay a similar charge against Irish patriot Roger Casement after the failed 1916 Rising. In publishing Casement's diaries showing his use of male prostitutes in his postings throughout the British Empire, authorities suggested that such exploitation and lack of control illustrated Irish nationalism's unsuitability for self-government. It also forced Casement into a political limbo for over fifty years after his execution, as investigations into the authenticity of the diaries remained disputed.

The social meanings attributed to male prostitution were taking place within the context of wider discussion about women, sexuality and prostitution in Ireland and Europe. In Ireland, in the nineteenth century women who worked in prostitution were seen as conduits of venereal disease, and as such, they were perceived as a grave risk to both the military capacity of the nation and the moral boundaries of the family unit. This moral panic culminated in the Contagious Diseases Acts (1864, 1866, 1869) which gave the police and the medical profession extensive jurisdiction over the female body to examine, to label and if necessary, to incarcerate (Walkowitz 1980: 1; McCormick 2009: 4). Male prostitution, by contrast, was seen as phenomena that resided outside wider society by a minority of clearly identifiable 'perverts' (Scott 2003: 181). In the twentieth century too, during both World Wars, the danger prostitution posed to the nation emerged again leading to renewed attempts to regulate, punish, classify, rescue or treat women whose behaviour was seen as culpable (McCormick 2009: 5). Prostitutes and sexually active working-class women were seen as most at most at risk (p. 112). Within a society that viewed women as being of a higher moral standing than men, those that transgressed from these lofty expectations were more severely punished. Prostitution in Ireland had been seen as a consequence of having large military garrisons of British soldiers based in towns throughout the country (Luddy 2007: 25). Women servicing this demand were seen as sexual traitors to an imagined construction of Irish womanhood. With the advent of independence, prostitution, unsurprisingly remained a feature of the independent state prompting Catholic moral purity movements like the Legion of Mary to campaign for the closure of brothels particularly in Dublin's Monto district between 1923 and 1925 (McCormick 2009: 28; Luddy 2007: 214; Howell 2003: 330).

Male Prostitution in the Twentieth Century

The discourse governing male prostitution would again change by the mid-twentieth century. In urban areas, bars and clubs frequented by gay men would also include young men who were looking for clients for commercial sexual encounters. These younger men became characterised often as drifters or hustlers; products of disruptive family backgrounds where low educational attainment contributed to a precarious life, leaving them vulnerable to being preyed upon by older gay men (Logan 2017; Scott et al. 2015). This seduction narrative proved especially popular in the 1950s when the USA became convulsed with panic about internal threats to the security and stability of the country with gay government officials seen as susceptible to blackmail from Communists (Kaye 2003: 22). The hustler architype became embodied as a masculine heterosexual ideal popular and desired amongst gay men, but also by a wider population disaffected by the strict conventions that governed traditional family life in the 1950s. The desire for a new countercultural masculinity found voice through the popularity of American actors like James Dean in his film performances like *Rebel without a Cause*, where a disaffected young men vulnerable to the corruption of urban living was a theme.

Research on male prostitution reflected those themes by locating commercial sex within a delinquency perspective focusing on the heterosexual street hustler as the principle supplier of transactional sex to gay men (Butts 1947; Ginsberg 1967), documenting a continued decline on the wider availability of 'trade' amongst poorer and other working-class men (Kaye 2003: 23). Reiss' (1961) now classic work on male prostitution in the USA identified the central traits of the social relations between young men and their male clients that took place in specific outdoor spaces in the urban community. Both participants understood the expectations that surrounded these social relations with the younger men socialised in the practice within peer groups that constituted, according to Reiss, 'lower-class delinquency' (1961: 109). The peer groups were socially organised and permitted their members to earn 'easy' income from prostitution but only under strict circumstances that rejected both the definition of hustler and homosexual (p. 112). Sexual activity was limited to oral sex and marked by 'affective neutrality'—a transitory transaction conducted and arranged through gestures with almost no words spoken. Other studies throughout the 1960s confirmed these elements of the social organisation of male prostitution and the threat of violence that existed if these norms were violated, although the young men remained viewed as victims rather than perpetrators (Benjamin and Masters 1964: 291; Scott 2003: 187). Their clients, frequently pathologised within research, were viewed as sex starved, ageing men who had coerced young men into sex (Hauser 1962: 50).

The emergence of gay liberation across Europe and the USA in the 1970s further shaped the social meanings attributed to male prostitution. As 'coming-out' became a political mantra for the gay movement, straight identified hustlers that had previously profited from gay men were increasingly viewed as in denial about their own sexualities. The ability of straight hustlers to reconcile the performance of their heterosexuality and the limited range of sexual services they offered with, what Kaye (2003: 36) describes as, the 'new desires and subjectivities' of the gay movement became increasingly untenable. Gay men were casting off effeminate stereotypes of the past and embracing the hyper-masculinity that only hustlers had previously offered. Gay men were increasingly buying sex from other openly gay men. Some gay men derived pleasure and power from selling sex to others disrupting the construction of victim narratives. The meanings and motivations around male prostitution diversified with a typology of categories of street, escort and 'kept boys' established, while a new victim category of the middle-class runaway emerged (Weisberg 1985; Scott 2003; Kaye 2003). The advent of HIV/AIDS located male prostitution within a medical discourse where it was constructed as a public health concern bringing the body under the surveillance of government agencies. Through the institutional links forged between gay and lesbian communities and

government health officials, male sex work emerges as almost an exclusively gay phenomena, benefiting from increased campaigning by the
gay community (Scott et al. 2015: 85). A large body of research has
continued however to emphasise the deviant (Luckenbill 1986) and
pathological (Sargarin and Jolly 1997) nature of male sex work.

Research on Male Sex Work in Ireland

Changes to the organisation of male sex work over the last thirty years
have seen a dramatic rise in the numbers working indoors and online
(Scott et al. 2015: 87). Despite this, scholarly research has continued to
focus on street work, with Ireland being no exception. Greater availability of research funding towards projects that focus on sex work solely
within a context of drug dependency, sexual abuse or homelessness have
provided useful insights into the experiences of the most marginalised.
There has been, however a neglect of research within the indoor sector.

In Ireland, a number of projects on male prostitution published
between 1997 and 2004 share similar key findings. Firstly, there is a
focus on the *clandestine and stigmatized* nature of prostitution with the
INMAP (2001: 12, 31, 42) report dedicating a section on the 'underground nature of male prostitution'. The report, which focused on
service provision (2001: 31), argues there is a reluctance to identify as
someone selling sex for fear of 'slaggings or beatings' from their peers,
creating challenges for researchers and service providers alike in accessing such a hidden population. There is an additional assumption here,
similar to that of the 1950s seduction narrative research discussed earlier, that many of the men involved in prostitution are in fact identifying as heterosexual. In the McCabe et al. (2011) study, only one out of
12 participants identified themselves as gay while INMAP (2001: 41)
recognised that gay identified services would be off-putting to many
men involved in prostitution. Kearins (2000: 21) similarly asserts that
'many of the rent boys I met identified as heterosexual and vehemently
denied any homosexual tendencies'. Kearins (2000: 14, 20) also suggests that the 'underground nature of the profession' makes it impossible to accurately determine the numbers involved, which she speculates,

based on interviews with service providers, could be anything between 100 and 600 men.

Secondly, these projects reveal remarkably *similar backgrounds* of those involved in prostitution. The Quinlan et al. (1997: 28) study identified homelessness and drug abuse as important influences on the entry of men into prostitution, also reflected by the McCabe et al. (2011: 1000) study, that reported on the dysfunctional family backgrounds of their respondents, many having experienced physical and sexual abuse as well parental alcohol dependency. Kearins (2000: 23, 27) similarly identified her respondents as 'working class' with most citing 'homelessness (poverty), unemployment, drug/alcohol abuse, poor family backgrounds' as their motivation for engaging in commercial sex.

Thirdly, there is limited data on the *impact of migration* on male sex work during the period 1997–2004, with the exception of Carroll and Quinlan's (2004) study looking at six men, characterised as either migrants, refugees or asylum seekers, who accessed sexual health services in Dublin. Just one of these men identified as a male sex worker, claiming it was easier than his experience in the UK, given that there were fewer non-drug using sex workers in Dublin (p. 12). The traditional lack of focus on migration in many studies (e.g. Kearins 2000) is unsurprising. The social and economic transformation of Ireland from the mid-1990s resulted in different stages of inward migration; from returned Irish migrants in the 1990s, increased non-EU migration from 2002–2004 and movement of people from the EU accession states in 2007 (Gilmartin and White 2008).

The Rise of Neo-Abolitionism

The stories in this book are told against the backdrop of a high-profile political and civil society campaign to reform existing prostitution laws in Ireland. The founding of the Immigrant Council of Ireland (ICI) in 2001 with funding from the Religious Sisters of Ireland would mark a turning point in the institutionalisation of neo-abolitionism in civic and political life. ICI embarked upon a campaign to introduce a law, similar to one passed in Sweden in 1999 that criminalised the purchase of sex (Levy 2015). This campaign would have three dimensions—alliance building, evidence gathering and parliamentary engagement. Firstly, ICI lobbied for the support of a wide range of organisations, including political parties, state feminist organisations, trade unions and professional organisations to support their call for a change in the law that would see the introduction of a sex purchase ban. In conjunction with Ruhama, an organisation founded by the Good Shepherd Sisters and the Sisters of Our Lady of Charity, that helps women who are victims of exploitation and trafficking within prostitution, this broad alliance became known as *Turn off the Red Light* (ToRL) (Ryan and Ward 2017: 51). Secondly, ICI sought to provide intellectual leadership to support legislative change, commissioning research framed within a neo-abolitionist understanding. The report rejected any distinction between prostitution and trafficking (ICI 2009: 1), claimed that agency and choice were not relevant concepts and argued that, based on the analysis of escort websites, one thousand women were working in prostitution each day in Ireland. Thirdly, the ToRL campaign sought political engagement, lobbying individual politicians and parties to bring independent motions for legislative change, forcing the government into a commitment to establish a review of prostitution policy (Ryan and Ward 2017: 52). Ward has argued that even before this public consultation by the Joint Committee on Justice, Defence and Equality (JCJDE) had taken place, the political debate was in effect over, with the main political parties accepting ToRL's definition of the problem and it's solution (Ward 2017: 87).

Organisations and interested individuals were invited to make written submissions to the JCJDE of which a number would be asked to make presentations in an oral hearing. The dominance of the neo-abolitionist perspective led to an almost exclusive focus on the Nordic model of client criminalisation, with civil servants from Sweden invited to give testimony before the JCJDE committee, while no alternative policy alternatives were discussed, e.g. decriminalisation in New Zealand. The JCJDE also embarked upon a fact-finding trip to Sweden but again failed to visit or consult with officials from any alternative European country offering an alternative model of regulation of sex work (Ward 2017: 94). In the public hearings, 13 out of the 15 groups that spoke supported the policy of client criminalisation, with organisations like the Irish Nurses and Midwives Organisation (INMO) conflating trafficking and voluntary economic migration in their presentation (FitzGerald and McGarry 2016: 299). The INMO assumption that no migrant woman from a developing country could give consent for her involvement in prostitution, as opposed to the 'voluntary' sex work of white, Western women, is central to understanding how knowledge about the sex industry has been constructed, often through a racialised lens. It should be noted that the INMO testimony and that of the Irish Medical Organisation (IMO) ran counter to the advice of global organisations like the World Health Organisation (WHO) and UNAIDS who have advised member countries not to impose further criminalisation of sex work (Fitzgerald and McGarry 2016: 296).

The JCJDE findings were no surprise, with the committee recommending the introduction of client criminalisation, increased penalties for trafficking and making the act of accessing websites advertising prostitution illegal. The testimony of prostitution survivors was specifically identified by the JCJDE as being persuasive evidence in their final report. The passage of the *Criminal Law (Sexual Offences) Act 2017* saw the enactment of key JCJDE recommendations, including the criminalisation of the purchase of sex. The act did not decriminalise the seller of sex completely; workers remained criminalised with increased penalties if they were found to have sold sex together under brothel keeping laws and were also criminally liable under loitering laws.

The Stories in This Book

The stories in this book are taken from interviewees that were undertaken with 18 self-identified gay men from Brazil and Venezuela between March 2015 and September 2017. They were aged between 19 and 27 and were engaged in some form of commercial sexual activity. This age group was slightly younger than the male sex respondents in the Sanders et al. (2018: 59) study, where the largest cohort was aged 25–34 years old. All the men, bar one, had entered on a stamp two student visa and as such demonstrated access to €3000 prior to arrival and were studying either at college or university or were attending a recognised English-language school. The study's sample was recruited primarily through the gay dating site PlanetRomeo, which has a dedicated escort section, and then through the process of snowball referrals from existing contacts.

The focus on South American escorts, specifically Brazilian and Venezuelan, emerged from their prominence on the dating site's escort section; out of 84 escorts advertising in March 2015, 41 identified as either Brazilian or Venezuelan with a further 16 as identifying their ethnicity as 'Latino' though not specifying their nationality. The role of ethnicity in the construction of the participants' online self-identity varied. As countries of inward migration, the skin colour of the Brazilian and Venezuelan escorts I interviewed often reflected their mixed race heritage with most choosing—Latin, Black or Mixed from pre-selected ethnicity categories available on the site. The role of this racialised construction of the men's online profile is discussed further in subsequent chapters. I conducted the interviews by an in-depth qualitative approach through English, although the information sheet and consent form given to participants were translated into Portuguese and Spanish. A payment of €50 was offered to the participants of which fourteen availed of and four declined. I interviewed five participants a second time and continued to follow them on social media. The names used in the book are pseudonyms. At the time of interviewing, the English-language competency of the participants ranged from elementary to proficient although the data reveal the difficulties encountered by them as they entered sex work upon their arrival in Ireland with limited English-language skills often reliant on applications like Google translate in online conversations. They were highly competent using new social media and digital platforms and as such, their migrant status did not place them at a disadvantage working in online sex work as suggested in the Sanders et al. (2018: 3) study. Additional data in the book is drawn from field notes taken during 20 sessions of participant observation in a gym identified by my respondents as being a location where they socialised and had made contact with sexual partners and clients.

I entered into these interviews as a supporter of a harm reduction approach to sex work and through my role on the board of a sex work advocacy project, Sex Workers Alliance Ireland. I have outlined elsewhere the difficulties faced by researchers of the sex industry in a time of contentious politics (Ryan and Huschke 2017) and the challenges of positioning oneself as the researcher within feminist inspired sexuality research (Ryan 2006).

Once I had established contact with respondents from these online sites, they directed me to their more frequent use of Grindr and Instagram. I analysed these profiles by following a number of the men's accounts, but I have not reproduced photos from the content of those accounts, as my initial consent did not extend to the use of photographs and subsequent attempts to gain consent for the use of redacted photos was refused.

Notes

1. http://www.ruhama.ie/. I use the term prostitution to describe policy, historical events or when it is known to be an organisation's preferred terminology. I use the term sex work to describe my research respondents as it includes a broad range of activities within the sex industry including camming, stripping, sugar daddy relationships and face-to-face commercial sex. See Sanders, T., O'Neill, M., & Pitcher, J. (2009). *Prostitution: Sex work, policy & politics* (pp. 5–12). London: Sage for a good overview of terminology and its uses.
2. Federal authorities in the USA shut down rentmen.com in 2015. Its chief executive was sentenced to six months in prison for the promotion of prostitution the following year.
3. While participants in this book discuss how they use Grindr to initiate the sale of sexual services, it should be noted that Grindr's Community Guidelines explicitly state that 'Profiles advertising sexual services (including escort or massage services) will be banned'. Grindr's Terms and Conditions also ban the sale or advertising of goods and services. See https://www.grindr.com/terms-of-service/ and https://www.grindr.com/community-guidelines/ Instagram similarly bans the 'sale of sexual services' in its Community Guidelines. See https://help.instagram.

com/477434105621119. Participants in this book discuss ways in which they attempt to subvert in-app features to market sexual services in ways unintended by social media networks.
4. http://uk.businessinsider.com/instagram-monthly-active-users-1-billion-2018-6?r=US&IR=T. Accessed July 26, 2018.
5. https://www.irishtimes.com/business/economy/ireland-forecast-to-record-highest-gdp-growth-in-europe-this-year-1.3562629?mode=sample&auth-failed=1&pw-origin = https%3A%2F%2Fwww.irishtimes.com%2Fbusiness%2Feconomy%2Fireland-forecast-to-record-highest-gdp-growth-in-europe-this-year-1.3562629. Accessed July 23, 2018.
6. The Labouchere Amendment to the Criminal Law Amendment Act 1885 outlawed gross indecency between me, effectively criminalising all homosexual activity made punishable by up to two years hard labour (Weeks 1996: 48).
7. *United Ireland* was the leading nationalist newspaper founded in 1881 by Charles Stewart Parnell under the editorship of William O'Brien where it was the voice of the tenant reform organisation; the Land League founded by Michael Davitt but had become a fierce critic of every aspect of the colonial presence in Ireland (Lyons 1990: 173).

References

Allen, K. (2000). *The Celtic Tiger: The myth of social partnership*. Manchester: Manchester University Press.
Barry, K. (1995). *The prostitution of society*. New York: New York University Press.
Batty, M. (1997). Virtual geography. *Futures, 29*(4/5), 337–352.
Bauman, Z. (2000). *Liquid modernity*. Cambridge: Polity Press.
Benjamin, H., & Masters, R. E. L. (1964). *Prostitution and morality: A definitive report on the prostitute in contemporary society and analysis of the causes and effects of the suppression of prostitution*. New York: Julian Press.
Berg, H., & Penley, C. (2016). Creative precarity in the adult film industry. In M. Curtin & K. Sanson (Eds.), *Precarious creativity: Global media, local labor*. Oakland: University of California Press.
Bourdieu, P. (1986). The forms of capital. In J. E. Richardson (Ed.), *Handbook of theory of research for the sociology of education*. Westport: Greenwood Press.

Brennan, J. (2017). Cruising for cash: Prostitution on grindr. *Discourse, Context & Media, 17*, 1–18.

Brents, B. G., & Sanders, T. (2010). Mainstreaming the sex industry: Economic inclusion and social ambivalence. *Journal of Law and Society, 37*(1), 40–60.

Butts, W. M. (1947). Boy prostitutes of the metropolis. *Journal of Clinical Psychopathology, 8,* 673–681.

Carroll, D., & Quinlan, M. (2004). *Kinda project: Young migrant men in prostitution.* Dublin: Gay Men's Health Board and East Coast Area Health Board.

Chauncey, G. (1994). *Gay New York: Gender, urban culture and the making of the gay male world, 1840–1940.* New York: Basic Books.

Daroya, E. (2018). 'Not into chopsticks or curries': Erotic capital and the psychic life of racism on Grindr. In D. W. Riggs (Ed.), *The psychic life of racism in gay men's communities* (pp. 67–80). London: Lexington Books.

De Souza e Silva, A. (2006). Mobile technologies as interfaces of hybrid spaces. *Space & Culture, 9*(3), 261–278.

Featherstone, M. (2010). Body, image and affect in consumer culture. *Body and Society, 16*(1), 193–221.

Fitzgerald, S., & McGarry, K. (2016). Problematizing prostitution in law and policy in the Republic of Ireland: A case for reframing. *Social and Legal Studies, 25*(3), 289–309.

Giddens, A. (1991). *Modernity and self-identity: Self and society in the late modern age.* Cambridge: Polity Press.

Giddens, A. (1992). *The transformation of intimacy: Sexuality, love and eroticism in modern societies.* Cambridge: Polity Press.

Gilmartin, M., & White, A. (2008). Revisiting Irish contemporary migration: New geographies of mobility and belonging. *Irish Geography, 41*(2), 143–149.

Ginsberg, K. N. (1967). The meat-rack: A study of the male homosexual prostitute. *American Journal of Psychotherapy, 21,* 170–185.

Graham, M., Hjorth, I., & Lehdonvirta, V. (2017). Digital labour and development: Impacts of global digital labour platforms and the gig economy on worker livelihoods. *Transfer, 23*(2), 135–162.

Hauser, R. (1962). *The homosexual society.* London: Bodley Head.

Hindmarch-Watson, K. (2012, July). Male prostitution and the London GPO: Telegraph boys' "immorality" from nationalization to the Cleveland Street scandal. *Journal of British Studies, 51*(3), 594–617.

Howell, P. (2003). Venereal disease and the politics of prostitution in the Irish free state. *Irish Historical Studies, xxxxviii*(131), 320–341.

Hubbard, P., Matthews, R., & Agustin, L. (2008). Away from preying eyes? The urban geographies of 'adult entertainment'. *Progress in Human Geography, 32*(3), 363–381.

Immigrant Council of Ireland (ICI). (2009). *Globalisation, sex trafficking and prostitution: The experience of migrant women in Ireland.* Dublin: Immigrant Council of Ireland.

Irish Network Male Prostitution (INMP). (2001). *Such a taboo.* Dublin: Irish Network Male Prostitution and East Area Health Board.

Jones, A. (2015). For black models scroll down: Webcam modelling and the racialisation of erotic labour. *Sexuality and Culture, 19,* 776–799.

Kaye, K. (2003). Male prostitution in the twentieth century: Pseudohomosexuals, hoodlums homosexuals and exploited teens. *Journal of Homosexuality, 46*(1/2), 1–76.

Kearins, E. (2000). *Rent: The secret world of male prostitution.* Dublin: Marino Books.

Khamis, S., Ang, L., & Welling, R. (2017). Self-branding, 'micro-celebrity' and the rise of social media influencers. *Celebrity Studies, 8*(2), 191–208.

Kitchin, R., & Dodge, M. (2011). *Code/space: Software and everyday life.* Cambridge, MA: MIT Press.

Levy, J. (2015). *Criminalising the purchase of sex: Lessons from Sweden.* London: Routledge.

Logan, T. D. (2017). *Economics, sexuality and male sex work.* New York: Cambridge University Press.

Luckenbill, D. F. (1986). Deviant career mobility: The case of the male prostitute. *Sociology, 33,* 283–296.

Luddy, M. (2007). *Prostitution and Irish Society 1800–1940.* Cambridge: Cambridge University Press.

Lyons, F. S. L. (1990). *Ireland since the famine.* London: Fontana Press.

MacPhaill, C., Scott, J., & Minichiello, V. (2015). Technology, normalisation and male sex work. *Culture, Health and Sexuality, 17*(4), 483–495.

Maginn, P., & G. Ellison. (2014). Male sex work in the Irish Republic and Northern Ireland. In V. Minichiello & J. Scott (Eds.), *Male sex work & society* (pp. 426–461). New York: Harrington Park Press.

Mahdavi, P. (2010). Race, space, place: Notes on the racialisation and spatialisation of commercial sex work in Dubai, UAE. *Culture, Health & Sexuality, 12*(8), 943–954.

Marwick, A. E. (2013). *Status update: Celebrity, publicity and branding in the social media age*. New Haven: Yale University Press.

Marwick, A. E. (2015). Instafame: Luxury selfies in the attention economy. *Public Culture, 27*(1), 137–160.

McCabe, I., Acree, M., O'Mahony, F., McCabe, J., Kenny, J., Twyford, J., et al. (2011). Male street prostitution in Dublin: A psychological analysis. *Journal of Homosexuality, 58*, 998–1021.

McCormick, L. (2009). *Regulating sexuality: Women in twentieth-century Northern Ireland*. Manchester: Manchester University Press.

McLean, A. (2013). 'You can do it from your sofa': The increasing popularity of the internet as a working site among male sex workers in Melbourne. *Journal of Sociology, 51*(4), 889–902.

Mosse, G. L. (1985). *Nationalism and sexuality: Respectability and abnormal sexuality in modern Europe*. New York: Howard Fertig.

O'Connor, M., & Healy, G. (2006). *The links between prostitution and sex trafficking: A briefing handbook*. Brussels: CATW and European Women's Lobby.

Ó Riain, S. (2014). *The rise and fall of Ireland's Celtic Tiger: Liberalism, boom and bust*. Cambridge: Cambridge University Press.

Page, R. (2012). The linguistics of self-branding and micro-celebrity in Twitter: The role of hashtags. *Discourse & Communication, 6*(2), 181–201.

Patterson, M., & Elliott, R. (2002). Negotiating masculinities: Advertising and the inversion of the male gaze. *Consumption Markets & Culture, 5*(3), 231–249.

Paul, J. P., Ayala, G., & Choi, K. H. (2010). Internet sex ads for MSM and partner selection criteria: The potency of race/ethnicity online. *Journal of Sex Research, 47*(6), 528–538.

Quinlan, M., Wyse, D., & O'Connor, A. M. (1997). *Men in prostitution*. Dublin: Gay Men's Health Project and Eastern Health Board.

Reiss, A. (1961). The social integration of queers and peers. *Social Problems, 9*(2), 102–119.

Robinson, B. A. (2015). 'Personal preference' as the new racism: Gay desire and racial cleansing in cyberspace. *Sociology of Race and Ethnicity, 1*(21), 317–330.

Rojek, C. (2001). *Celebrity*. London: Reaktion Books.

Ryan, P. (2006). Researching Irish gay male lives: Reflections on disclosure and intellectual autobiography in the production of personal narratives. *Qualitative Research, 6*(2), 151–168.

Ryan, P. (2016). #Follow: Exploring the role of social media in the online constructions of male sex worker lives in Dublin, Ireland. *Gender, Place & Culture, 23*(12), 1713–1724.

Ryan, P., & Huschke, S. (2017). Conducting sex work research in a politically contentious climate: Lessons from Ireland. In A. King, A. C. Santos, & I. Crowhurst (Eds.), *Sexualities research: Critical interjections, diverse methodologies and practical applications.* London: Routledge.

Ryan, P., & Ward, E. (2017). Ireland: The rise of neo-abolitionism and the new politics of prostitution. In S. Jahnsen & H. Wagenaar (Eds.), *Assessing prostitution policies in Europe.* Milton Park: Routledge.

Sanders, T., O'Neill, M., & Pitcher, J. (2009). *Prostitution: Sex work, policy & politics.* London: Sage.

Sanders, T., Scoular, J., Campbell, R., Pitcher, J., & Cunningham, S. (2018). *Internet sex work: Beyond the gaze.* Cham: Palgrave.

Sargarin, E., & Jolly, R. W. (1997). Prostitution: Profession and pathology. In L. B. Schlesinger & E. R. Revitch (Eds.), *Sexual dynamics of anti-social behaviour.* Springfield: Charles C. Thomas.

Scott, J. (2003). A prostitute's progress: Male prostitution in scientific discourse. *Social Semiotics, 13*(2), 179–199.

Scott, J., MacPhail, C., & Minichiello, V. (2015). Telecommunications impacts on the structure and organization of the male sex industry. In P. Maginn & C. Steinmetz (Eds.), *(Sub)urban sexscapes: Geographies and regulation of the sex industry.* London: Routledge.

Senft, T. M. (2008). *Camgirls: Celebrity and community in the age of social networks.* New York: Peter Laing.

Van Dijck, J. (2013). 'You have one identity': Performing the self on Facebook and LinkedIn. *Media, Culture & Society, 35*(2), 199–215.

Van Doorn, N. (2017). Platform labor: On gendered and racialized exploitation of low-income service work in the 'on-demand' economy. *Information, Communication & Society, 20*(6), 898–914.

Van Krieken, R. (2012). *Celebrity society.* London: Routledge.

Walkowitz, J. R. (1980). *Prostitution and Victorian society: Women, class and the state.* Cambridge: Cambridge University Press.

Walsh, M. J., & Baker, S. A. (2017). The selfie and the transformation of the public-private distinction. *Information, Communication & Society, 20*(8), 1185–1203.

Ward, E. (2017). The Irish Parliament and prostitution law reform: A neo-abolitionist shoe-in? In E. Ward & G. Wylie (Eds.), *Feminism, prostitution and the state.* Abingdon: Routledge.

Weeks, J. (1996). The construction of homosexuality. In S. Seidman (Ed.), *Queer theory/sociology* (pp. 41–63). Cambridge: Blackwell.

Weisberg, D. K. (1985). *The children of the night: A study of adolescent prostitution*. Lexington: Lexington Books.

2

Discipline and Desire in the Pursuit of Physical Capital

Abstract In this chapter Ryan focuses on the role physical and erotic capital plays in the lives of male sex workers. The possession of smooth, muscular bodies correspond to a standardised, global template in many European societies and are deployed for social and economic gain. Drawing from Bourdieu (1986), Ryan illustrates how the body has a symbolic value and communicates discipline, taste and class location to others. The chapter shows how sex workers navigate body projects like the gym and how they provide an interface with their digital identities.

Keywords Physical capital · Bourdieu · Taste · Male sex work · Gym

Introduction

I am waiting in a café for my interview with Luan. He is a twenty-seven-year-old Brazilian national, who relocated to Ireland two years ago. Upon his arrival, he is immediately apologetic about his English—'when I arrived I spoke nothing, nothing, I learned English in seven months' he tells me, blaming his public school education for this crash

© The Author(s) 2019
P. Ryan, *Male Sex Work in the Digital Age*,
https://doi.org/10.1007/978-3-030-11797-9_2

course in the language he has experienced since his arrival. Luan is rightly proud of his progress and has funded his relocation to Ireland himself. He tells me of sitting alongside some of his fellow Brazilian students who are financially supported by their parents, who have enjoyed the benefits of private, high school education and whose English language competency extramural classes and trips to Florida improved. It is often the first time they have sat in a classroom with fellow nationals from very different socio-economic locations from themselves. This diversity continues amongst the men that I interviewed. They grew up in different parts of Brazil and Venezuela, had a range of educational and professional backgrounds and arrived in Ireland with varying levels of financial resources to sustain them until they entered employment. Their motivations for their entry into sex work are also diverse. Drawn into the flexible and opportunistic nature of the work, facilitated by social media apps, their involvement can be either sporadic—to pay a deposit for an apartment, or more continuous in funding foreign travel, better accommodation and their social life. Some stories are finite—their departure date is set, while others hope to investigate means, which will enable them to remain within Ireland, by pursuing further educational training or applying for a European Union passport.

These students, who entered sex work, are united by the physical capital they brought to Dublin's gay scene. In this chapter, I argue that while the men may come from different backgrounds, their smooth and muscular bodies represent a global, standardised template that has become idealised and fetishised within European gay culture. The stories in this chapter will trace the realisation of this physical capital within the men's lives and the potential it held for conversion into economic and social opportunities. The discussion is influenced by the work of Pierre Bourdieu. I understand the body as a bearer of symbolic value, an unfinished product, which is subjected to self-discipline, which is gazed upon and has become objectified and commodified in this advanced consumer society. The body represents an embodied cultural capital—social skills, habits and tastes—accumulated over time, skills that live within, and die with the holder (Bourdieu 1986: 48). The body communicates discipline—and desire—to others, in how it is dressed, fed and maintained. In this chapter, I explore the *habitus* of the men I have interviewed—the systematic approach to their diets, aided by fitness apps to calculate calories, the cultivation of an optimum body size and the maintenance of the body's hair and colour.[1] I discuss how the homogeneity of a Western bodily ideal in gay culture may have largely erased evidence of the class body, but illustrate how the men still read signs that enabled them to identify class location through, tattoos, for example. Ultimately, the men learned how the capital they accumulated through body projects like the gym, where the body was showcased, could invite conversion into economic advantage.

The Changing Body Within Irish Culture

The body has traditionally played a central role within Irish culture. Since the foundation of the state in 1922, Catholic social teaching became woven into the legislative fabric of the nation, leading to prohibitions enacted against contraception and divorce and limiting access to material deemed sexually explicit, through restrictive censorship laws (Ryan 2012: 16, 65; Ferriter 2009: 386). Throughout the nineteenth century, the body was subject to penance, self-denial and fasting, becoming an important means by which the faithful highlighted their religious devotion. It was a process where civility and morality were embodied to enable the modernisation of Irish society through the discipline of past generations (Scheper-Hughes 1979: 123; Inglis 1998: 157). Religious orders and their deployment in schools to oversee the segregation of the sexes, impressed upon children the values of modesty and chastity, where the body became a site of temptation and sin becoming, in Tom Inglis' words, 'an object of private guilt and public shame' (Inglis 1998: 156). This private, internalised moral code contributed to wider demographic trends such as postponed marriage, high marital fertility and permanent celibacy, trends that have become synonymous with an international reputation that viewed the Irish, somewhat dubiously, as 'troubled by sexuality' (Scheper-Hughes 1979: 97).

The Catholic Church's construction of the body as a site of modesty and self-denial began to unravel in the second part of the twentieth century, as Ireland slowly moved from a traditional, rural conservative society to a more modern, industrial and secular one. A generational shift in political leadership brought about a challenge to the economic insularity and social conservatism of the past, ushering in the embrace of the free market, where state incentives saw American and European firms establish bases in Ireland (Garvin 2004: 33). This new investment was fuelled by an expansion within education that was committed to the creation of a new labour force that could adapt to the needs of a modern economy (Lee 1989: 326) and take advantage of the single market opportunities available upon Ireland's membership of the European Economic Community in 1973. Catholic social teaching was increasingly contested in the 1960s and 1970s. Second wave feminist campaigns targeted legislation prohibiting contraception both inside and outside parliament, while gay rights organisations campaigned against the continued criminalisation of homosexuality. Changing tastes in music and fashion liberated young people from the formal dance hall rules of their parents' generation, allowing them the freedom to move their bodies to music and in clothing that would eventually bring the era of modesty and self-restraint to a close (McCourt 1992: 20–21).

A new ethic of liberal individualism started to emerge in Ireland in the latter half of the twentieth century, encouraged by a growing industrial, urban and secular society (Inglis 2004: 137). Citizens become autonomous individuals competing against each other in a marketplace of work and leisure. Sociologists have explored these changes characterised as high, late, post or liquid modernity, which have charted the rise of individualism and consumerism (Giddens 1991; Beck 1992; Bauman 2001). Young people were now freer from the ascribed identities of their birth—religion, class, family and ethnicity—and led more individual, autonomous and rational lives. Young people were tasked with the creation of their own moral compass, to determine right from wrong in a society where, in Beck's (1992: 88) words made them the 'the centre of their own planning'. Rather than practising self-denial, the self itself was to become an ongoing, reflexive project. This path to self-realisation would rely upon choosing from a myriad of resources to advise and coach, so that the individual could become the author of his or her own life (Giddens 1991: 5).[2] It was this ethic of individual fulfilment that would become the strongest mandate in late modern societies (Beck and

Beck-Gernshein 2002). Bauman argues that seeking these resources, made readily available by consumer capitalism, would become an obsessive pursuit in itself. Promising to be recipes for a successful life, these consumer possibilities would come with a 'use by' date as they are replaced and updated by new and improved competitors (Bauman 2000: 72). For Bauman (2000: 72), in this consumer race, 'the finishing line always moves faster than the fastest of the runners'. Life becomes endless 'shopping around' for the skills and possessions that convince ourselves, and others, that we are reaching our full potential. For Giddens (1991: 81), these possessions represent patterns of consumption with habits governing modes of dress, food and behaviour that constitute the 'material form to a particular narrative of self-identity'.

The body is also representative of these material forms, where individuals deemed fat, unfit or ageing before their time are, as Featherstone (2010: 195) argues, seen as 'not only slothful but as having a flawed self'. The pressure to embrace this ethic of transformation has become core to consumer culture and within late modernity itself—where a range of experts, from personal trainers to stylists, stand ready to support this 'before and after' makeover, at a price. There has also been an increased visibility of the male body in cinema and advertising that has further accelerated the practice of the body becoming a key site of identity performance in this late modern age. For Giddens (1991: 102), we have become 'responsible for the design of our bodies', where we can exercise control in an increasingly individualised and uncertain world. These bodies require maintenance to stay healthy but also to pursue the more nebulous concept of fitness. Bauman (2000: 78) suggests that fitness is a subjective or felt experience, one with no natural end. Targets to achieve fitness are never ending. The pursuit to achieve them is characterised by 'self-scrutiny, self-reproach and self-deprecation', leading to a state of perpetual anxiety.

The Meaning of Muscles

The pursuit and display of bodily athleticism are not new. The gymnasium has had a central role in ancient Greek society (Alvarez 2008: 25), while concerns over masculinity, fitness and military readiness amongst

European powers in the nineteenth century led to the expansion of school gymnasiums (Andreasson and Johansson 2014: 95; Bonde 2003: 96). The rise in popularity at this time of strong-men contests focusing on brute strength gave way to wider audiences for bodybuilding, focusing on the body's aesthetic value (Alvarez 2008: 37–45). Bodybuilders like Eugene Sandow became famous touring the USA with crowds gathering to see and touch his body, while the advent of photography allowed his image to be mass-produced around the world, creating a market for images of the body that defied strict indecency laws (Andreasson and Johansson 2014: 96). Political and religious leaders also harnessed this popularity in fitness as a way to stem a moral panic over the perceived declining physical and moral health of the nation. Diseases like syphilis were associated with medical conditions such as miscarriage, stillbirth and post-natal abnormality, leading organisations like the British Eugenics Education Society to question the unchecked procreation of the physically and morally unfit (Hall 2000: 66–69). Bodybuilder Charles Atlas was also motivated by a similar fear in the nation's declining physical health and contributed to the growth of this 'muscular Christianity' in the USA (Andreasson and Johansson 2014: 97).

Economic and social transformations throughout the twentieth century redefined the embodiment of male workers across class and racial lines. Labour histories reviewed by Ava Baron reveal how working-class men incorporated the muscularity of their bodies into protest when confronted with technological change or by the increasing number of women in the workforce (Baron 2006: 147). The muscular male body became valorised as a perquisite for many working-class occupations like printing, constructions and streetcars, bolstering the creation of a heroic masculinity, deemed under threat from technology and a creeping feminisation within society. These bodies would also be subject to the gaze of others. While deriving cultural capital within specific communities where muscular bodies were in public view and in clothing that emphasised the body, there was also a corresponding trend amongst the middle classes to conceal it. Kasson's (1990) study of manners in nineteenth-century urban America traces the development of the popularity of suits amongst middle-class men, designed to shield the body from public gaze. This concealment allowed the middle-class male white body to remain—white—in contrast to ethnic minorities or those that laboured in the sunshine, illustrating Baron's (2006: 149) view, that 'muscularity served to empower or disempower depending upon the angle of the gaze'. Middle-class men would also embrace muscularity in the early twentieth century, just as technological developments made its deployment in the labour market largely obsolete.

By the 1980s, bodybuilding culture would become more mainstream, popularised by athletes like Arnold Schwarzenegger and the movie *Pumping Iron*. Andreasson and Johansson (2014: 99) locate its rise in a Reagan-Thatcher political era, where culture wars were fought over the jurisdiction of the body in areas such as abortion and HIV/AIDS. Controversy over anabolic steroid use and the often disapproving gaze upon bodybuilders by a mainstream society who thought such exaggerated muscularity to be disproportionate contributed to the sport remaining a subculture (Monaghan 1999: 281). While the mesomorph body shape may well be the masculine ideal in Western society (Thompson and Cafri 2007), it must also be developed within a normative understanding of the emerging fitness industry as opposed to bodybuilding culture. This fitness industry offered clients gyms or, more frequently called, health clubs with a wider variety of equipment, from traditional weights to aerobic fitness machines. This new constituted gym is associated with increasing female memberships and a move from being spaces of discipline to, with the incorporation of swimming pools, massage and nail bars, spaces where the body is pampered (Leeds Craig and Liberti 2007: 684; Andreasson and Johansson 2014: 104). The gym has been spatially reconstructed to accommodate these new elements, while there has been a global standardisation of the bodily ideals, equipment and fitness regimes like BODYPUMP to attain them (Parviainen 2011: 527; O'Toole 2009: 76; Johansson and Andreasson 2016: 150).

Body Projects in a Late Modern Age

While I discussed earlier Bauman's dire prediction of the consequences that a lifetime of surveillance of the body's shape and fitness will bring, it has not deterred the pursuit of muscularity, which has grown exponentially. In Britain, the number of 16–25-year-olds going to the gym has increased from 14.7% in 2006 to 21% in 2013, while the gym and fitness magazine *Men's Health* has become the biggest selling men's magazine (Hakim 2018: 232). This has increasingly become a global phenomenon with the fitness industry generating an estimated $75 billion in revenue in 2012 (Johansson and Andreasson 2016: 144). Brazil, from where the majority of my interviewees were born, ranks second only to the USA in the size of the revenue generated by health and fitness clubs. In a number of European countries, there has been a decrease in young people's (aged 16–29) participation in team sports and a corresponding increase in individualised sports in fitness centre settings (Pedersen and Tjornhoj-Thomsen 2017: 431). In Denmark, for example, 44% of 16–19-year-olds and 40% of 20–29-year-olds had participated in strength training on a regular basis in the last year. The development of the body within the newly constituted fitness industry in the 1990s would have particular resonance for gay men. The images of bodybuilding and fitness had, since the nineteenth century, operated as a form of homoerotica with magazines, like *Physical Culture*, widely read amongst gay men throughout the 1940s and 1950s, in a time of sexual repression in the USA (Benzie 2000: 161). This 'proto-porn' may have been recast by the violent hyper masculinisation in the movies of Schwarzenegger and Stallone in the 1980s, but gay men were about to re-appropriate the gym as a key source of cultural capital, where the body would become a central expression of identity.

Emerging from the catastrophe of the AIDS crisis, which continued to claim thousands of lives throughout the 1990s, the extension of the fitness industry resonated with gay men eager to embrace the pursuit of a muscular body and disassociate themselves from the sickness connotation of the thin body (Benzie 2000: 164). The pursuit of this muscular body would serve a political purpose too, declaring a war upon the gay effeminate stereotypes that had haunted gay men for generations, a war against effeminacy that has continued to this day. It was a body that would be more masculine than those of the straight men who had taunted those who were gay, or perceived to be (Bronski 1998). Gay pride had an embodied dimension in which the muscular male body communicated to the world the discipline and self-control of the holder, in line with late modern social practices (Duncan 2010: 440).

Within these cultural contexts, hierarchies exist in which different male body shapes have been located—the mesomorph, or athletic build at the top with the endomorph or larger build, at the bottom. For gay men, the cultural capital attached to specific body types has, of course been naturalised much earlier within educational contexts for example, but become magnified within gay culture where the body both communicates sexual desire and is a beacon for the desires of others. Drawing from Bourdieu, I understand gay culture or the 'scene' as a *habitus*, where judgements about taste are exercised and where cultural capital is accumulated. The status a man has within gay culture is dependent on the different forms of capital he has accumulated—for example, having the economic capital to buy an expensive home or car but also the cultural capital to exercise taste and discernment in choosing the right wine or indulging in current food trends. This exercise in discernment or the pursuit of *distinction* exists not merely in the accumulation of knowledge or objects, but extends to the body itself. Bourdieu (1986: 48) identifies this embodied dimension of cultural capital (in addition to objectified and institutionalised), stating that 'in its fundamental state, it is linked to the body and presupposes embodiment'. The body becomes a source of physical capital, the bearer of status and power which can be converted into other forms of capital, like economic and social (Shilling 2003: 111). For Bourdieu, bodies bear the imprint of social class, derived from their economic location and habitus with its associated development of taste (Bourdieu 1984: 190). I return to these themes in Bourdieu's work later in the chapter to use my interviewees' stories to illustrate how they have converted their physical capital in diverse ways. I will also argue that contemporary gay culture, in which these men operate, has facilitated the flattening of the social class imprint upon the body through the standardisation of consumer body practices that constitute this habitus.

Fitness 365 Gym

The gym played a major role in the lives of the men I interviewed. Early conversations clearly identified one Dublin city centre gym as popular with migrant gay men, particular from South America. I re-joined this gym in June 2015 (I had previously been a member two years before), which I have called Fitness 365 in the book, and attended three times a week over the following year. I have incorporated field notes taken from a diary during this short ethnographic piece of my research into this chapter, illustrating how my respondents' online and offline lives intersected in locations like the gym.[3] The gym is accessed through a small laneway off a busy thoroughfare in central Dublin. Upon entering, you walk upstairs into a large room, which is furnished with red velvet curtains, sofas and armchairs and the reception desk and then through doors to a traditional gym layout of cardio machines, weights and separate spaces for fitness classes. Downstairs houses the changing rooms, a 25-metre swimming pool, sauna and steam room, all decorated in black and gold mosaic tiles. Five lounger style chairs surround the pool with three TV screens built into the walls. There were nine separate memberships available to purchase, including student and off-peak membership, which was the most common amongst the men that I interviewed.

All eighteen men in the study had previously held gym memberships prior to moving to Dublin, while for the majority they had joined the gym within three weeks of their arrival. This interest was motivated for some by previous experience of physical education at school, although the availability of sports facilitates like running tracks, swimming pools and exercise equipment varied greatly across regions and whether schools were private or public. Gustavo (22), currently taking a year off from university in Brazil, described the cultural differences in the importance of physical education stating that—

> I used to do gymnastics in school and gym work in school since I was 14 or 15, it is what I do, and I can't imagine not going to the gym – what do you guys do in Ireland? *(laughs)* I mean even the skinny guys are fat in Ireland, skinny with big belly, uggh it is so weird, I hate to look.

Men that I interviewed, particularly from Brazilian coastal cities, like Florianópolis and Rio de Janeiro, emphasised the role of the beach in their lives, where it was both a means to get fit and an incentive to maintain their fitness. Leo (25) describes the role of the beach in his life prior to his arrival in Dublin—

It was a lot of time, most days; everyday at the beach … in summer it is high 30s so most days after work my friends would meet there when it was cooler, still in our clothes from work. At the weekends, I played volleyball there, every weekend for years. Do you play? You do not need a gym if you play; I never think about it as 'working-out', it was fun and you got really fit … All my happy times were there [the beach], with my family and especially with my grandfather. I miss it so much.

Bruno, a twenty-one-year old chef, also felt that Brazilians, particularly in coastal cities, had different cultural attitudes to the body and the gym compared to Irish men, which encouraged their investment in body projects like the gym, tanning and hair removal.

It is different for us, in my city I can walk in a speedo four blocks from the beach and nobody looks; it's normal, the Irish in the changing room are strange, like their body should be hidden more, maybe they are shy? No? It's all towels and showering in their underwear … I work hard on my body and I enjoy showing it off; I wear t-shirts – like this one – that makes me look good, what problem is this? Guys look at me in the gym, they come up and talk to me, want to add me to Facebook (*laughs*) I like it.

The majority of men recognised that being good looking and having a muscular body held advantages both in their native countries but also in Ireland. Luan (27), from Brazil, spoke of having experience from both perspectives, that of an overweight child and adolescent until sixteen and then as young adult who committed to attending the gym five days a week to achieve a dramatic transformation of his body.

It was difficult for me as a child because I was bigger than my friends … I was fat, I can show you photos, I was 86kgs … being at the beach I always had a t-shirt on, even swimming, I said I would go red from the sun but that wasn't true, I was very ashamed of my body. Now, it is crazy because I can't keep my shirt on (*laughs*) in all my photos! But the gym saved my life and I feel so much more confident and people know that, I see how people look at me now, I was invisible and now I'm not, people look at me, even my college professor I remember, she was always looking at me, always so friendly, not when I was fat, people buy me drinks in bars now.

Others also identified the 'bodily dividend' that was secured in the gym. Victor (25) told me how he was struggling to find work as a waiter in Dublin until a friend gave him 'the list', which helped him secure work.

> The list! Well yes, it was given by a friend in my class to me and it was a list of restaurants, six restaurants or cafés I think and he told me that the managers only hire guys that they think are good looking and I should try and the first one – a week probation and she hires me, after searching for two months, the first one … and I am really bad *(laughs)* no really, I'm not good but they like me, I'm friendly and I smile a lot even when I make mistakes, then it is good again.

All respondents in the study recognised the value of a more muscular body in improving their confidence, reflecting a correlation between realising a stable self-identity through the relationship with their bodies (Crossley 2006: 42). The quotes from the Brazilian men growing up in coastal cities recognise the role of the beach as a public space where the body is both trained and displayed to others. This role the beach as a public space has also been identified in similar studies in Australia (Johansson and Andreasson 2016: 154). All these accounts recognise the presence of bodily or physical capital (Bourdieu 1984; Wacquant 1995) where time and energy invested into the building a muscular body can be later exchanged for economic, social and cultural capital. There has been considerable research that has identified the importance of physical capital in specific professions or social fields that value the body, like modelling (Mears 2011), athletes (Paradis 2012) and personal trainers (Frew and McGillivray 2005; Hutson 2013). I am arguing, however, that my interviewees reveal the scope of physical capital and its exchange value to be much wider, located within workplaces, universities and within the habitus of the gay male social scene. This embodied form of capital is important within advanced consumer societies that demonstrate a strong aestheticisation of everyday life, where the body is validated not for what it can do, but what it looks likes (Frew and McGillivray 2005: 163). Physical capital only holds this symbolic value in social settings or, in Bourdieu's terms, fields, where it is held in high esteem enabling it to be traded successfully. Victor's story of the six potential workplaces where management were thought to hire only good-looking staff reflects the commercial value that employers placed on aesthetic labour. This form of labour, manifested in physical characteristics, is leased by the holder and commodified by the labour process to provide 'a 'style' of service encounter deliberately intended to appeal to the sense of the customers' (Nickson et al. 2003: 185). Studies do show that good looks, intelligence and personality do impact on earning potential for both men and women (Judge et al. 2009). Other interviews, including Victor, felt that this aesthetic labour was also appreciated by customers who complemented his smile—'I do well in tips, it's the smile, I just keep smiling … but to be serious, really, it is the t-shirt, [points to it] never wear a large or extra-large'. Here, Victor alludes to the t-shirt he wears in the café where he works, the same one he is wearing when I meet him for his interview for this book, prior to going to his shift. Indeed, it is smaller and well fitted for a man of his size.

The Fitness 365 gym was the main site where this physical capital was achieved for most of my respondents, although some had left to join cheaper alternatives in the city. The importance of the gym in the men's lives was threefold—it was their sole exercise activity since they arrived in Dublin, most had greater time to attend than their previous lives in Brazil and Venezuela would permit and finally, it was social, where they would go and workout with their friends. My field notes from the gym reveal copious references to this social element of attending the gym, including this example—

Field notes—Fitness 365—19.30 h

> There are three guys now loitering at the rope pull down machine, one which is using it while the others block the adjacent one – are they using it? It is busy today and people occasionally stop and look in the direction of the guys, but nobody has yet asked them are they using it. They are talking in Portuguese while they are standing there – all three look remarkably similar, in height and body, muscular guys no doubt. One is wearing what appear to me yoga pants while the others are in shorts and singlets, definitely not needed in Spring especially if you are working out … so one of the guys on reception desk has joined them for a

chat, I know this guy well, he is Brazilian he always remembers my name, though he seems to remember everyone's name and I'm not so sure how to pronounce his name, never seen that before, no idea how he does that remembering trick, he goes back to the reception desk after 5 minutes, he says hello as he passes by.

This social dimension had also been identified in Denmark by researchers Pedersen and Tjornhoj-Thomsen (2017: 438) who found that while the gym is an individual pursuit, members did go with friends or made social relationships with people in the gym. This created a culture where heterosexual men would support each other in their workouts, looking and commenting on the bodies of their friends and finding training solutions to help their friends reach their fitness goals. The researchers locate this ease with looking and having your body subject to the gaze of others to the rise of the distribution of gym photos on social media sites like Instagram, a topic I return to in detail in Chapter 4. Similarly, research in Scotland by Frew and McGillivray (2005: 166) found the acceptance of being gazed upon by others in the gym as 'openly accepted, even celebrated … in an apparently asexualized and agendered way'. While this was also obviously a characteristic within Fitness 365, there is the potential to move this gaze of admiration amongst gay men, into either a commercial or a non-commercial sexual encounter. I understand this bodily display by male sex workers in the gym as a platform or as a showroom for encouraging conversation, social media followers and prospective sexual encounters.

Sexual Encounters in the Gym

The reference in my notes to Portuguese speaking staff was also mentioned by several respondents who joked that it was the easiest administrative task that they completed in Dublin and was a factor in which gym they chose to join. Although respondents recognised the social aspect of the gym, they also acknowledged it had the potential for sexual encounters. All 18 men I interviewed said they had been directly propositioned for sex in either the gym, changing rooms or showers or the possibility of sex had been implied to them. Thiago (21) and Luan (27) explain this common experience—

> I think it is at night mostly, before closing, but it happens, it is not a problem for me. Guys leave the [shower] door open if they are interested, or use no towel in the changing room. I'm not shy in the gym, but I concentrate on myself, the workout, I see guys watching sometimes or they come over to talk. One guy came over and chatted but I didn't talk much with him and then he say – 'how much?' He knows nothing about me! It upset me – he never would have said that to an Irish person. (Thiago, 21)
>
> I have seen it in the sauna, there is a lot of cruising going on for guys, they are in the pool, the shower, then sauna and repeat it – it is easy to find, I prefer this to grindr, in my city [Sao Paulo] you just meet people on the street or the gym, it is natural, I am really bad on Grindr, face to face is best for me, No one has their own room here – I share my room with 3 guys, maybe that's why they have fun [sex] in the gym? (Luan, 27)

My own field notes confirmed both Thiago and Luan's experiences in the gym, where the pool area and sauna were clearly an area of the gym to see and be seen by others. These areas appeared to be almost exclusively male when I attended, particularly in the evening, and confirmed the role of muscularity in the ability to 'pick-up' men for sexual encounters (Drummond 2005: 279).

Field notes—Fitness 365—20.00 h

> Came downstairs from the gym which was really busy, as is changing room, 15-20 people, mostly changing and going home, at the pool there are two guys speaking Portuguese on the loungers, one showering in the area near the pool, where I am. They are all wearing speedo swimwear, they disappear for a while, I think to the sauna and later the steam room which is in my view – the guys on the loungers are on the phones … about twenty minutes later one of them is taking a photo of their friend in the open shower which has gold mosaic tiles.

While all of my respondents had been sexually propositioned, directly or indirectly, few had recruited clients directly or had paid sexual encounters in the gym. An exception was Lucas, a 24-year-old Brazilian student who described how he had used Grindr and the gym as an entry to sex work upon his arrival in Ireland. The use of applications like Grindr has been identified as facilitating sexual hook-ups by gay men in the gym (Gudelunas 2012: 357), and in the quote below, we see the use of the app facilitating commercial sex.

> I spoke no English really, a few words then and with no job and so much extra time, I went to the gym six days a week maybe … the first guy I met was on Grindr when we were both in the gym and we chatted and another day I met him in reception, I asked him if he wanted some fun and how much he would give … that time he gave me €50 and we showered together.

Sometimes there was not a direct exchange of money. Renzo (23), a Venezuelan national described approaching a man who he had observed watching him on a number of occasions at the gym.

> *Renzo*: I had seen this guy in the changing rooms a few times, I think he waited around for me because he was so slow getting changed, he was tall, I'd say in his 40s I think, attractive too but he had a boyfriend. Maybe … I asked him if he wanted to go for a drink and we went to a bar and then to a steakhouse on the Green [St Stephen's]. That was it, just that, I like dinner and drinks.
> *Paul*: But what if he asked you to divide the bill, how did you know he would pay?
> *Renzo*: I know and he know. I have never paid anything on a date. Ever.

As I discuss in the next chapter, Grindr became a means to advertise commercial sex, as Lucas did, though the use of photos and emojis that communicated his potential interest. For the majority of the men, the gym was used to showcase their bodies and cultivate potential clients, some of whom may have spoken to them directly or watched them from afar. Rodrigo (24) describes how a number of clients described how they 'saw him at the gym' a number of times before they messaged him while others, like Rafael (26), told how he encouraged meeting men in the gym through social media posts—

> I did write it on my Grindr, telling guys where I worked out, and that they can come up and say, hello if they saw me, occasionally I put the times I was there and they do, it is about your profile so that people know who you are.

Reading the Body for Class Location

While all of my respondents saw gym work as an integral part of their daily lives to maintain the bodies which they had worked for years to cultivate, they also recognised them as essential to attract potential clients. There was unanimous agreement that the possession of a muscular body was essential to participate in male sex work, more important than having an attractive face. Furthermore, a majority of respondents felt that in Ireland this body type was more highly desired than in other countries, because of its rarity amongst men on the gay scene.

> Dublin is different, because there is no club culture you see no fit guys here, guys keep their shirts on in clubs, it's different from other places I have seen … it is good for us [sex workers] because they can't meet guys like me every day – on Grindr most gym guys are open to [sex] work. (Bruno, 21)
>
> The gyms are full here but Irish guys are still have not a good shape, maybe just foreigners go? In Brazil I'm just an average guy but in Dublin guys think I'm super-hot because I go to the gym – it's good for me. (Rodrigo, 24)

Some men I interviewed suggested that the emphasis on muscular bodies amongst Irish clients had allowed men to enter sex work who otherwise would be deemed unattractive, especially in home countries.

> Irish love muscle guys, we call them Barbies in Brazil, it is not a good, sometimes the body takes from the face, you understand? I see guys

working here and I am – how do people see it as attractive – a great body, ok! But with a face of the favela?! Irish don't see this, but I do. (Rafael, 26)

This reference to the favela by Rafael was one of a number made by the Brazilian men, which alluded to class and regional differentiation between them. The men recognised that Irish people tended to homogenise the Brazilian community, knowing little about the differences within the Portuguese language, the ethnic diversity or the regional disparities, particularly between the north and south of the country. Bruno (21) joked that he thought some Irish people thought that 'we are swinging from the trees' in Brazil.

Within Bourdieu's discussion of physical capital, there is an acknowledgement that the body is a site of power, class and social reproduction and bears the imprint of the individual's class location. Bourdieu (1986: 188) states that—

> It follows that body is the most indisputable materialization of class taste … It does this in the seemingly most natural features of the body (volume, height, weight) and shapes … its visible forms which express in countless ways a whole relation to the body, i.e., a way of treating it, caring for it, feeding it, maintaining it.

There are three determinants on the social formation of the body. Firstly, the *social location* or class position of the individual, which Rafael refers to above, suggests that the experience of poverty and associated structural inequalities literally becomes imprinted upon the face. A life of financial hardship and stress that can be read facially by others. Victor (25) goes further, stating that on Brazilian beaches, when the body is stripped of clothes that can act as cultural signifiers, he reads social class through the health of men's teeth. He explains that he uses it to assess whether 'I can feel safe, because you need to be watching for danger'. The premise of his observation is based on the popularity of expensive orthodontic treatment such as crowns, veneers and whitening, amongst the middle classes. Victor (25) admitted that his parents had spent considerable money in correcting his teeth.

The second determinant is the *habitus*; beliefs and attitudes taught to children to enable them to navigate social life where they become embodied in taste and consumption. For gay men, these skills are learned in peer groups, strongly influenced by digitally mediated advertising within a wider consumer context. For Bourdieu (1984: 190), how people treat their bodies reveal 'the deepest depositions of the habitus'. Four features emerge from the men I interviewed that give an insight into elements of this bodily habitus, which reflect class location and the social field of gay culture. Firstly, *bodily size*. While clients desired a muscular body, my respondents were conscious of an ideal size that was proportionate to their height and most desirable amongst their peers. Crucially, following Bourdieu (1986), I argue that while some treatment of their bodies does reflect class location, this ideal size was not a determinant of social class. The men I interviewed came from a range of social backgrounds, some had attended private school, others public, while they had all pursued further training and education, from prestigious universities to training colleges. While others, like Johansson and Andreasson (2016: 149) have argued that a global standardisation of the ideal body shape and the equipment used to achieve it has occurred, in what they describe as a McDonaldization process, I am suggesting that this standardisation is incredibly pronounced with mainstream gay culture.[4] In the eighteen men I have interviewed, there is remarkably little difference in their body size. As Gill et al. (2005: 40) describe—

> We are witnessing an extraordinary fetishization of muscles and muscularity in young men at precisely the moment that fewer traditionally male manual jobs exist, and those that do require less physical strength than ever before. Highly developed muscles have become 'semiotically divorced' from specific class connotations, and are no longer indexical of participation in manual labour.

Unlike Bourdieu's (1984: 211) statement below, there was, in fact agreement on all three 'profits' that the men in my study, irrespective of class location, were achieving. It is to these extrinsic profits that I return to in the next chapter.

It can be easily shown that the different classes do not agree on the profits expected from sport, be they specific physical profits, such as the effects on the external body, like slimness, elegance or visible muscles and on the internal body, like health and relaxation; or extrinsic profits such as social relationships a sport may facilitate, or possible economic and social advantages.

Thiago (21) describes how at just 1.68 cm, he is afraid of getting too big—'my friends say if I look at weights [dumbbells] I gain muscle, it is very easy for me but too easy if I overtrain I get too big and it looks bad ... if I post these photos, a few love them but more hate, in my [sex] work guys won't choose me'. Rodrigo (24) also felt that being too big was undesirable and describes how he previously lost perspective on the size of his own body—'You see the results and you want more and more, then a guy comes up in a bar and says 'fuck you are huge' but his face is not one that wants you, he thinks you are weird, not good for my [sex] work'. Monaghan's (1999: 279–280) bodybuilding respondents had also felt conscious of an alternative gaze from the general public when they left the gym which saw them as looking 'ridiculous'. Achieving and maintaining this optimum size became a challenge for most of the men in my study.

Secondly, *body hair*. All of the men, bar one, I interviewed removed body hair on a regular basis. This primarily involved shaving chest hair, highlighting particularly the abdominal muscles, although a minority of respondents also removed hair on the legs and buttocks.[5] Hair removal is identified in other studies of male escorts (e.g. Walby 2012: 153), although niche markets exist for escorts with body hair that identify as 'bears'. While Walby (p. 152) stresses in his study of Internet escorts in the USA that there is no one ideal body type, I argue that there was an overwhelming uniform body type advertising online during my research, which was Latin/white, muscular and hairless.

Gustavo (22): I used shave my chest and ass but with razor, it is not always so good ... I did laser treatments, which are good but expensive ... €500 each for six times.

Lucas (24): Before I would not shave in winter in Ireland but for [sex] work, you need to shave all year, guys expect it, so I do it.

Thirdly, *tattoos*. The use of tattoos has been identified as a means to tell stories and to 'speak' to others about the values and identity of the bearer. While tattoos have a long history within criminal and countercultural movements, they are one of a number of body modifications increasingly embarked upon by individuals in late modernity as they seek to construct their biographies, often using the medium of their own bodies to do so (Kosut 2000: 80). The public visibility of many tattoos holds the potential to influence our social interaction as they are also read by others as we navigate everyday life. A majority (12 out 18) of my respondents had, at least one tattoo, and these ranged both in size and their visibility. Some men expressed judgement about the tattoos of others, suggesting certain designs indicated a lower class location, while others told how they feared their tattoos were off putting to potential clients.

> *Luan (21)*: I love my tattoo, it is on my back, you can see here [lifts up his t-shirt] but it is big isn't it? … I was always interested in India and the spiritual culture so I decided on Ganesh [the Hindu God] … some people love it, one guy told me I was being rude and it was not a good thing to use … In my photos I never show my back because I think some guys [clients] won't contact me if they see it.
>
> *Bruno (21):* These guys with the star tattoos and the three birds' ones, you know, they are so bad, so bad, when I see them I know I step back and these guys are working in Ireland? Maybe the men they meet, the Irish don't care or don't know?

Finally, *skin colour*. The men I interviewed often commented that they were now, unsurprisingly, paler since their arrival in Ireland from Brazil or Venezuela. They lamented the loss of their darker skin, which they saw as embodying health, showcasing their bodies and making themselves more sexually desirable to potential clients and to partners for non-commercial sex and dating. Skin colour, and to a lesser degree eye colour, was a key point of differentiation for the men I interviewed. They all believed that this was central to their popularity on both the gay dating scene and amongst sex work clients, a belief confirmed by their success when they travelled on 'tour' to cities like Zurich and Vienna.

Guilherme (27): Everyone wants the opposite, right? I love blue eyes, they [Irish people] love brown eyes, they want what is different and strange to them – they are pale and hairy and so they want smooth, darker guys, fit guys. You give them what they want.

   Leo (25): They [clients] also say oh you have beautiful eyes; oh, your skin is so beautiful. In Brazil, nobody says this, everyone has dark eyes … being dark is OK, but not too dark, you know, my friend worked in Dublin and he is from Salvador and is a dark, mixed guy and he says guys don't like, the nordestinos [north easterners] aren't as popular.

Gregory Mitchell's (2015: 57) study of straight-identified male sex workers in gay saunas in Brazil also found that the process of racialisation was uneven and context specific. Local Brazilian, and some Western clients, often rejected black sex workers in favour of lighter skinned or moreno [brown skinned] ones. All sex workers were part of a discourse of hypersexuality but black men often had to perform an exaggerated macho persona to attract clients (2015: 34). Similarly, I interviewed a man who had advertised his nationality as Venezuelan, who during the course of the interview admitted that he had in fact being born in Romania. Given that he could speak Spanish and had some family members living in Madrid, he changed how he advertised himself online, attracting more clients as a result. 'No one wants to fuck a Romanian' he told me.

The third determinant on the social formation of the body is *taste*. This refers to lifestyle preferences that impact upon the body and are located within economic constraints. For Bourdieu (1986: 187), food is a clear example of how taste impacts upon the 'strength, health and beauty' of the class body. Drawing from his extensive study of class and food tastes in France, Bourdieu suggests that the working classes have a greater concern with the strength rather than the shape of the body, eating cheap and nutritious food as opposed to the more health-conscious middle classes. Again, there is evidence of a standardisation in the food consumed by the men in my study, unsurprising given the reliance on social media and global magazine chains like *Men's Health* for nutritional advice. The preparation and consumption of food displayed an extraordinary discipline. Most men I interviewed, utilised an application like *MyFitnessPal* which enabled them to calculate and weigh their nutritional needs for the day, broken down into protein, carbohydrates, fibre, sugar and fat. While foods from their native Brazil and Venezuela did feature, these were often referred to nostalgically, associated with family meals, most often cooked by their mothers or grandmothers.[6] Within an Irish context, they were foods that were reserved for a special occasion, given they were often time-consuming to prepare. The Brazilian dish of *feijoada* was the most commonly referred to; a beans, beef and pork dish that requires many hours to cook and didn't feature in the everyday food diaries men kept on their phones.

> *Gilherme (28)*: I miss feijoada so much, it is not the same taste here, there is a restaurant here that I tried, I have never made it at home … a girl in my class started to make coxinhas and bring them to class, it was money for her, everybody loved them and her … thinking about food makes me want to go home, I miss home.
>
> *Thiago (21)*: I buy my food every weekend, I try and make food for every day but I have many guys in my house and the kitchen is small … this week I made food at 1am because it was quiet – like chicken, tuna and beef dishes.
>
> *Renzo (23)*: I use plastic boxes for my food during the day so I can eat three times during the day, I don't want to eat bad when I am here [Dublin].

Hakim's (2018: 235) study of gym work and social media also revealed respondents who, like Renzo spent an hour each morning cooking nutritious individually boxed meals to be eaten during the day. While the gym has been discussed as an individualised body project (Gill et al. 2005: 57; Crossley 2006: 42), the preparation of food was no less individual, with men rarely eating collectively with their flatmates, except at the weekends. Increased food costs, which in addition to the purchase of supplements like creatine and whey protein, constituted a significant financial commitment each week.

Conclusion

This chapter used the stories of gay men recently arrived from Brazil and Venezuela to argue that the cultivation, maintenance and display of the body within spaces popular with the LGBTQ community, yielded a physical capital. The dividend was accrued, because the men embodied an idealised shape that has been gazed upon, fetishised and commodified in Western consumer societies. Upon arrival in Ireland, these men realised their bodies had a higher physical capital, and potential exchange value, than they had in their countries of origin. Their bodies, the product of fitness regimes started within schools and honed in sports played with family and friends on beaches in coastal cities, were considered more exceptional than their paler local counterparts.

Drawing from Bourdieu, I have argued these men internalised preferences in eating, exercise and fashion that have become a *habitus* which is both a way of living for the men I interviewed and crucially, becomes an aspirational handbook for other gay men. This desire to achieve a similar muscularity or covet those who possess it, opens up opportunities for sexual encounters, both commercial and non-commercial. While habitus maybe class-based, I have argued that the homogenisation of the desired body type within LGBTQ communities and the global standardisation of workout plans, diet and supplements have greatly reduced the imprint of class upon the body. This is exaggerated in the stories of men I have interviewed because the gym has overwhelming become the sole form of sport and exercise that the men have engaged in since their arrival. Even still, within these stories, men tell of 'reading' each other's bodies for indicators of class through tattoo design, accent, dental work and facial appearance. In the next chapter, I focus on how these bodies become digitally mediated through dating applications like Grindr, exploring the selection of photos and how they are read by others to invite commercial sexual opportunity.

Notes

1. Following Bourdieu (1986: 241), I am using capital to refer to those resources that 'are accumulated human labour' and hold the potential to produce forms of reward. Types of capital include economic (income, monetary assets), cultural (skills, knowledge), social (connections) and symbolic (status).
2. Lash (1994: 120) is critical of Giddens over the extent to which people can reflexively construct their lives without acknowledging the influence of the person's socio-economic location. Bagguley (1999: 72) similarly argues there is a neglect of power and social inequality in Giddens' work with his concept of reflexivity being too individualistic.
3. I drew upon field note taking guidelines from Emerson et al. (2011). Loic Wacquant (2007) has written, perhaps, the most famous gym ethnography. See also Trimbut (2011) and Crossley (2006), for examples, of gym ethnographies.
4. The McDonaldization thesis is associated with George Ritzer (2011) *The McDonaldization of Society*. London: Sage. On the impact of globalisation on habitus see A. Appadurai (1997) *Modernity at Large*. Minneapolis: University of Minnesota Press.
5. Mitchell's ethnographic study of Brazilian garatos or 'straight' escorts working in gay saunas also show a preference for shaving to showcase the muscular body (Mitchell 2015: 11).
6. Food memories are a central theme identified by Cairns et al. (2010: 600) in their study on food, gender and class.

References

Alvarez, E. (2008). *Muscle boys: Gay gym culture*. New York: Routledge.

Andreasson, J., & Johansson, T. (2014). The fitness revolution. Historical transformations in the global gym and fitness culture. *Sports Science Review, XXVIII*(3–4), 91–112.

Appadurai, A. (1997). *Modernity at large*. Minneapolis: University of Minnesota Press.

Bagguley, P. (1999). Beyond emancipation? The reflexivity of social movements. In M. O'Brien, S. Penna, & C. Hays (Eds.), *Theorizing modernity: Reflexivity, environment and identity in Giddens' social theory* (pp. 65–82). London: Longman.

Baron, A. (2006). Masculinity, the embodied male worker, and the historian's gaze. *International Labour and Working-Class History, 69*(1), 143–160.

Bauman, Z. (2000). *Liquid modernity*. Cambridge: Polity Press.

Bauman, Z. (2001). *The individualized society*. Cambridge: Polity Press.

Beck, U. (1992). *Risk society: Towards a new modernity*. London: Routledge.

Beck, U., & Beck-Gernshein, E. (2002). *Individualization: Institutionalized individualism and its social and political consequences*. London: Sage.

Benzie, T. (2000). Judy Garland at the gym—Gay magazines and gay body building. *Journal of Media and Cultural Studies, 14*(2), 159–170.

Bonde, H. (2003). Masculine sport and masculinity in Denmark at the turn of the century. In S. Ervø & T. Johansson (Eds.), *Among men: Moulding masculinities, volume 1*. Burlington: Ashgate.

Bourdieu, P. (1984). *Distinction: A social critique of the judgement of taste*. Cambridge, MA: Harvard University Press.

Bourdieu, P. (1986). The forms of capital. In J. E. Richardson (Ed.), *Handbook of theory of research for the sociology of education*. Westport, CT: Greenword Press.

Bronski, M. (1998). *The pleasure principle: Sex, back lash and the struggle for gay freedom*. New York: St. Martin's Press.

Cairns, K., Johnston, J., & Baumann, S. (2010). Caring about food. *Gender & Society, 24*(5), 591–615.

Crossley, N. (2006). In the gym: Motives, meaning and moral careers. *Body & Society, 12*(3), 23–50.

Drummond, M. J. N. (2005). Men's bodies: Listening to the voices of young gay men. *Men and Masculinities, 7*(3), 270–290.

Duncan, D. (2010). Embodying the gay self: Body image, reflexivity and embodied identity. *Health Sociology Review, 19*(4), 437–450.

Emerson, R. M., Fretz, R. I., & Shaw, L. L. (2011). *Writing ethnographic fieldnotes*. Chicago: University of Chicago Press.

Featherstone, M. (2010). Body, image and affect in consumer culture. *Body and Society, 16*(1), 193–221.

Ferriter, D. (2009). *Occasions of sin: Sex and society in modern Ireland*. London: Profile Books.

Frew, M., & McGillivray, D. (2005). Health clubs and body politics: Aesthetics and the quest for physical capital. *Leisure Studies, 24*(2), 161–175.

Garvin, T. (2004). *Preventing the future: Why was Ireland so poor for so long?* Dublin: Gill and Macmillan.

Giddens, A. (1991). *Modernity and self-identity: Self and society in the late modern age.* Cambridge: Polity Press.

Gill, R., Henwood, K., & McClean, C. (2005). Body projects and the regulation of normative masculinity. *Body and Society, 11*(1), 37–62.

Gudelunas, D. (2012). There's an app for that: The uses and gratifications of online social networks for gay men. *Sexuality and Culture, 16,* 347–365.

Hakim, J. (2018). 'The spornosexual': The affective contradictions of male body-work in neo-liberal digital culture. *Journal of Gender Studies, 27*(2), 231–241.

Hall, L. A. (2000). *Sex, gender and social change in Britain since 1880.* Houndsmill: Macmillan Press.

Hutson, D. J. (2013). 'Your body is your business card' bodily capital and health authority in the fitness industry. *Social Science and Medicine, 90,* 63–71.

Inglis, T. (1998). *Moral monopoly: The rise and fall of the Catholic Church in modern Ireland.* Dublin: University College Dublin Press.

Inglis, T. (2004). *Truth, power and lies: Irish society and the case of the Kerry babies.* Dublin: University College Dublin Press.

Johansson, T., & Andreasson, J. (2016). The gym and the beach: Globalisation, situated bodies, and Australian fitness. *Journal of Contemporary Ethnography, 45*(2), 143–167.

Judge, T. A., Hurst, C., & Simon, L. S. (2009). Does it pay to be smart, attractive or confident (or all three)? Relationships among general mental ability, physical attractiveness, core self-evaluations, and income. *Journal of Applied Psychology, 94,* 742–755.

Kasson, J. F. (1990). *Rudeness & civility: Manners in nineteenth-century urban America.* New York: Hill & Wang.

Kosut, M. (2000). Tattoo narratives: The intersection of the body, self-identity and society. *Visual Sociology, 15*(1), 79–100.

Lash, S. (1994). Reflexivity and its doubles: Structure, aesthetics, community. In U. Beck, A. Giddens, & S. Lash (Eds.), *Reflexive modernization: Politics, tradition and aesthetics in the modern social order* (pp. 110–173). Cambridge: Polity Press.

Lee, J. (1989). *Ireland 1912–1985: Politics and society.* Cambridge: Cambridge University Press.

Leeds Craig, M. C., & Liberti, R. (2007). 'Cause that's what girls do': The making of a feminized gym. *Gender & Society, 21*(5), 676–699.

McCourt, H. (1992). *Oh how we danced*. Derry: Guildhall Press.

Mears, A. (2011). *Pricing beauty: The making of the fashion model*. Berkeley: University of California Press.

Mitchell, G. (2015). *Tourist attractions: Performing race and masculinity in Brazil's sexual economy*. Chicago: Chicago University Press.

Monaghan, L. (1999). Creating 'the perfect body': A variable project. *Body & Society, 5*(2–3), 267–290.

Nickson, D., Warhurst, C., Cullen, A. M., & Watt, A. (2003). Bringing the excluded? Aesthetic labour, skills and training in the 'new' economy. *Journal of Education and Work, 16*, 185–2003.

O'Toole, L. (2009). McDonald's at the gym? A tale of two curves. *Qualitative Sociology, 32*, 75–91.

Paradis, E. (2012). Boxers, briefs or bras? Bodies, gender and change in the boxing gym. *Body and Society, 18*, 82–109.

Parviainen, J. (2011). The standardization process of movement in the fitness industry: The experience design of Les Mills choreographies. *European Journal of Cultural Studies, 14*, 526–541.

Pedersen, P. V., & Tjornhoj-Thomsen, T. (2017). Bodywork and bodily capital among youth using fitness gyms. *Journal of Youth Studies, 20*(4), 430–445.

Ritzer, G. (2011). *The McDonaldization of society*. London: Sage.

Ryan, P. (2012). *Asking Angela Macnamara: An intimate history of Irish lives*. Dublin: Irish Academic Press.

Scheper-Hughes, N. (1979). *Saints, scholars and schizophrenics: Mental illness, in rural Ireland*. Berkeley: University of California Press.

Shilling, C. (2003). *Body and social theory*. London: Sage.

Thompson, J. K., & Cafri, G. (2007). *The muscular ideal: Psychological, social and medical perspectives*. Washington, DC: American Psychological Association.

Trimbut, L. (2011). Tough love: Mediation and articulation in the urban boxing gym. *Ethnography, 12*(3), 223–255.

Wacquant, L. (2007). *Body and soul: Notebooks of an apprentice boxer*. Oxford: Oxford University Press.

Wacquant, L. J. D. (1995). Pugs at work: Bodily capital and bodily labour among professional boxers. *Body & Society, 1*(1), 65–93.

Walby, K. (2012). *Touching encounters: Sex, work & male-for male internet escorts*. Chicago: University of Chicago Press.

3

Grindr, Hybridisation and the Life a Pop-Up Escort

Abstract Ryan explores how the gay dating app Grindr provides a digital platform to display the male sex worker body. Self-photography provides the raw material for Grindr profiles that facilitate the construction of a transient and opportunistic pop-up escort that communicated to potential clients through a new genre of photos, text and emoji. These regularly changed and targeted specific audiences. Ryan shows how Grindr creates new online/real time interfaces that generated both opportunities and dangers for sex workers.

Keywords Grindr · Pop-up escort · Hybridization · Male sex work

Introduction

Bruno worked as a chef in Brazil before coming to Ireland in 2015. He is twenty-one years old. As we settle down to talk in a city centre café, he places his iPhone on the table beside us, the screen bright with a series of online notifications. In the course of our conversation, he tells me of a habit, he has acquired of taking shirtless photos of himself in

© The Author(s) 2019
P. Ryan, *Male Sex Work in the Digital Age*,
https://doi.org/10.1007/978-3-030-11797-9_3

the changing rooms of clothing stores. Not all changing rooms are the same, he assures me. Some have better lighting. Some are larger than others. 'So where do all these photos end up?' I ask. Most are deleted he tells me, but some are sent to followers on Snapchat and Instagram Story or are chosen for his Grindr profile. The stories of the body projects, which I discussed in the previous chapter, now seek a platform, a showcase, a digital embodiment. This is at the heart of what I address in this chapter, focusing on the use of Grindr, although the men I interviewed do use multiple online applications. The photos that Bruno and other men have accumulated form the raw material of their digital identities. While people may admire them in the gym or in a bar from afar, these digital identities have a global reach. They traverse the city, opening up hybrid spaces, created by the interface of the online and real-time worlds in new neighbourhoods, new workplaces and new cities, as my interviewees travel for work or for pleasure. Their choice of photo, text or emoji are read by fellow users who decipher the hidden meaning that suggests either their availability as sex workers, or an ambiguity that suggests a potential exchange of sex or companionship for some economic gain.

I argue that it is the ease with which their photos can be uploaded and deleted which enable the emergence of this pop-up sex worker. My interviewees represent these workers, slow to embrace a sex worker identity, even slower to advertise on mainstream escort websites like rentboy.com, lest it confirms such an identity. In this chapter, the men's stories reveal how they draw upon sex work as a resource, facilitated by the subcultural prestige with which their bodies are held both by residents and visitors to Dublin. It is a resource that is deployed intermittently to solve short-term problems in housing and employment. It is deployed at specific times and durations to fund foreign travel, to purchase consumer durables and facilitate their attendance in clubs and parties where drug use is prevalent. Sex work is also a resource that contributes to the pursuit of long-term goals, to enable a new life in Europe or to support a return to the countries of their birth.

Gay Men, Dating and Sex

The Internet has revolutionised how gay men meet for sex, dating and relationships. The desire for men to have sex with other men has, however, created a landscape of spaces throughout history where sexual activity has taken place. Public spaces, like parks and lavatories, have played a significant role in bringing men who have sex with men together, facilitating brief sexual encounters that often transgressed age and class (Chauncey 1994: 179). For men who resided in cramped housing, public spaces offered the only available privacy—a feature common amongst working-class communities where much social life occurred on the streets. In New York City, Central, Battery and Prospect Parks became familiar cruising grounds at the turn of the twentieth century, where men would seek sex, but who would also socialise and develop friendships with men they encountered there (Chauncey 1994: 182). While police authorities responded with plain-clothes surveillance and harassment, sexual activity persisted moving to beaches like Coney Island in the hot summer months where men found others like themselves, seeking sex or companionship, on sands that were already heavily ethnically segregated. A complex of subcultural codes emerged to help men identify and make contact with each other in spaces throughout the city (p. 189). Movie theatres also became a popular location for men to meet, with one theatre on Sixth Avenue in Manhattan recording forty-five arrests for homosexual solicitation in 1921 alone (p. 196). The bathrooms of the city's expanding subway system, dubbed tearooms, also became a central meeting point for men and initiated further plain-clothes surveillance operations that resulted in prosecutions and imprisonment in a workhouse for thirty to sixty days (p. 198). The sexual activities of tearoom trade would become more widely understood, at least within academic circles, following the publication of Laud Humphreys' (1970) study of casual sexual encounters in a public bathroom in St Louis, Missouri. The book gained notoriety for its apparent breaches of ethical standards that exposed Humphreys' research participants to dangers of disclosure, although the use of deception in research was widespread at the time of the book's publication (Lenza 2004: 32). Within the Irish context, I had previously interviewed men coming out in the 1970s, who also documented the role of sexual encounters in public bathrooms as they grappled with their emergent sexuality (Ryan 2003). In Ireland, where there were limited gay social venues, public sexual encounters remained a feature of gay men's lives. One interviewee, Micheal, described that experience (Ryan 2003: 80)—'People don't really understand it, certainly not younger people, you can't see cruising for sex in toilets in today's light where guys are doing it for some sexual thrill ... when I was growing up there was literally no other place to meet guys'.

Edwards (1994: 99–102) identifies two public sex contexts—the informal, like a public toilet that is 'converted' into a site for sex, and the formal site of a bathhouse or sauna. Bathhouses have been a dominant feature of the gay community for over forty years. These spaces were created to cater for the erotic and social needs of men, providing public, semi-public and private spaces that offered men seeking anonymous encounters an environment that brought them protection from assault and harassment (Holmes et al. 2007: 275). Much of the earlier academic research has focused on the role bathhouses played as symbol of gay liberation (Delph 1978; Lee 1976; Styles 1979). Allan Bérubé's (2003) history of the bathhouse in the USA also identifies them playing a more central role than anonymous sex, in overcoming the isolation that was endemic for gay men and contributing to the legal protections that the civil gay rights movement would ultimately secure. The development of the gay bathhouse occurred at a time of rapid urbanisation in the early twentieth century that saw the slow transformation of formerly gay tolerant Turkish or Russian baths, co-opted into a new, exclusively erotic role (p. 34). Gay bathhouses emerged when there were few exclusively gay social venues available to gay men, and there was a steady decline in their use by the general population (Chauncey 1994: 211). There was little prostitution within bathhouses, with the entrance fees often being a disincentive for hustlers (p. 220), which facilitated a more social environment amongst cliental, than an exclusively sexual one. Law enforcement authorities were often ambiguous in their surveillance of bathhouses, seeing them as a preferable alternative in their fight against public sex, although police raids did occur, especially throughout the 1950s (p. 41). Often the lack of raids was the result of payments made to the police from what were successful commercial establishments, rather than any policy of non-interference (Chauncey 1994: 215).

The surveillance of bathhouses would return once again in the advent of the HIV/AIDS pandemic as public health officials (Holmes et al. 2007: 276; Woods et al. 2003: 57) targeted them. Bathhouses closed in large numbers in the USA, at least temporarily. In Canada however, no major city embarked upon a policy of bathhouse closure, following advice that these locations could be a site for HIV prevention and education (Woods et al. 2003: 67). Although contemporary research has been dominated by the correlation of bathhouse use and HIV transmission, studies like Binson et al. (2010: 586) do support findings that show a high proportion of safer sex practices. There has also been discussion of the disparity between HIV transmission rates amongst Latino and Black communities, compared to white men who have sex with men, although studies like Reisen et al. (2010: 702) didn't find a higher a likelihood of unprotected anal intercourse in bathhouses compared to private homes. Indeed, Woods et al. (2013: 84) found little interest amongst bathhouse staff to monitor the sexual behaviour of clients in public areas of the premises.

In the contemporary world, filled with sexual possibility, gay men are drawn to such public or semi-private spaces like bathhouses by fetish, rather than the necessity to seek sexual gratification. Even gay bars and clubs, not unlike the high street, have struggled to keep a loyal cliental in the face of online 'shopping' for dates and sex in city centres eager to gentrify older red light districts. These 'infrastructures of intimacy', as Kane Race (2015a) describes them, have enabled gay men to seek out sexual and romantic connection through a digital sexual revolution that has re-imagined historical understandings of community. Smartphone applications like Grindr, and other websites that offer geo-location capacities, have, however, been heavily critiqued for their suspected links to increasing rates of sexually transmitted infections (Rice et al. 2012; Burrell et al. 2012). The days of men seeking out spaces designated to be gay or 'gay friendly' with the explicit intention of meeting others has greatly reduced. These spaces have largely become locations to meet and socialise with friends, with the erotic potential remaining optional. Studies, like Rosenfeld and Thomas (2012), show that same-sex couples are overwhelming more likely to meet online, with 70% of their respondents having done so.

Location-based dating applications like Grindr, Scruff and Manhunt play multiple roles in the lives of gay men. These apps, like Grindr, offer men an online space that is layered upon a physical place as they move through the urban environment creating, in Blackwell's et al. (2014: 9) terms, a 'co-situational' experience. As gay men move through the city, a new community of men opens up to them that reflects a diverse class, age and ethnicity profile of different neighbourhoods. Grindr's infrastructure allows the user to choose from predesignated ethnic categories—or to choose none—or 'other' to circumvent the racial profiling of users (Jaspal 2017: 194). The mobility of users when they check in on their apps as they travel or commute, digitally turning neighbourhoods gay throughout the city, has been identified as a central feature of the technology (Stempfhuber and Liegl 2016: 61; Ahlm 2017: 369; Batiste 2013: 123). Although apps like Grindr are largely perceived as facilitating casual encounters, there is now a body of research which shows a more nuanced use of the technology. In fact, in neoliberal societies the advent of gay marriage and the valorisation of domesticity in an age of heteronormativity has resulted in a stigmatisation of those involved in casual sex (Jaspal 2017: 196; Ahlm 2017: 372). The stigma felt by research respondents encouraged them to change how they presented themselves on their online profiles and forced them to abide by 'interactional rules' when communicating with fellow users, downplaying their immediate sexual intentions. This tension in the presentation of the online self has been identified in Thompson-Bonner's (2017: 1661–1669) work, who has categorised Grindr profile photos as either *hypersexualised*—emphasising a muscular and toned body and—*lifestyle,* communicating to other users an interest in travel or culture, for example. An exception to this more nuanced understanding of gay dating app usage is Tziallas (2015) who believes the sexual motivation, rather than being downplayed, is in fact the key driver of Grindr's success. Tziallas (2015: 761) rightly believes the success of Grindr as an amateur porn platform is predicated upon the desire of users to share naked photos and to receive others in return in a process decidedly different from accessing thousands of such anonymous photos online. The difference is the proximity of the user in which this photo exchange takes place, but also I would add the context of 'knowing' this user and the potential to realise a sexual encounter based on the inter- action. The motivation of this exchange goes beyond the pursuit of sex. The demand for validation from other users of the discipline and time invested in the body is a strong driving force in the willingness to share photos of it digitally. It is the desire to exchange and seek validation of the body through an exchange of photos that has enabled male sex workers to so effectively navigate Grindr, drawing in potential clients who want to see more, and accumulating physical capital through the gaze of other users.

Male Sex Work Online

Male sex workers have been beneficiaries of apps, like Grindr that use geo-location capability. Ten years earlier, most sex workers were using sites like Gaydar, established in 1999 by a company called QSoft (Light et al. 2008: 305), that offered a gay dating and social network forum. It was hugely successful, with 4.2 million members worldwide in 2007, drawing in diverse advertising revenue keen to target new consumers. Male sex workers were charged a commercial membership rate to advertise their services and use escort-specific chat rooms (Light et al. 2008: 307). This mode of engagement with men selling sex was largely disembodied, where potential clients sat at their desktop com- puters perusing static photos of the available men (Roth 2014: 2115). Research by Lee-Gonyea et al. (2009) similarly seeks to explore the use of the 'personal computer' when reviewing male escort sites in the USA, although she does recognise the advent of instant messaging used by some agencies to facilitate real-time communication between clients and escorts. Pruitt (2005: 195) also offers an analysis of 12,262 escort profiles which revealed the work to be populated by overwhelming white men (89%), spread evenly across different age groups from eight- een to fifty, with 67.2% of men providing face photos in their profiles.

Using such methodologies to analyse escort profiles can be problematic, with double counting (men having more than one profile targeted at different client audiences) and inactive profiles rarely controlled for. McLean's (2013) qualitative interviews with 23 male sex workers are more revealing. They show how working independently online on sites like Gaydar reflected the recognised decline in street work and brothel and agency work amongst men and the preference for clients 'to come to them' rather than having to solicit for business (McClean 2013: 8). The escorts all cited greater levels of anonymity, autonomy and safety from their online work, while it was economically more profitable without having to deduct agency fees (p. 9). Similarly, in Parsons et al. (2004: 1025) study, men who had previously sought work offline in bars or agencies spoke of the advantages of attracting a different cliental that was less likely to be drunk or high and more likely to spend more time over dinner or on an overnight. Escorts still had to negotiate safer sex limits on or during the visit with some acting in the role of sex educators, warning their clients of unsafe sex practices.

Grindr

All major gay dating sites now have a GPS application similar to Grindr, including Hornet, PlanetRomeo and Scruff. Grindr was the most popular app amongst the men I interviewed, although many had profiles on other apps that they would use discontinuously or delete and then reinstall. Upon downloading Grindr, the screen opens to a cascade of the nearest hundred profile thumbnails dominated by a photo, organised according to their proximity to the user. Clicking on a profile opens to a screen displaying the photo which scrolls down to a headline text and age (e.g. looking for sex), then to a longer biographical text and finally to physical characters (Brubaker et al. 2016: 376). These include height, weight, body type, ethnicity, position, tribes, relationship status and looking for.[1] There is also a 'social links' facility which enables users to add their Instagram, Twitter or Facebook usernames to their profile. Since this study was completed, Grindr has introduced an option asking users to identify a gender and appropriate pronoun and also their HIV status and the date of their last test.[2] There is also facility to chat, favourite chosen profiles as well as to block and report them to an administrator. The chat function allows users to send text (or a voice note on the advertisement free subscription version), photos and their location. There are rules (no nudity, no sex toys, no advertising, no marketing sexual services and no revealing clothes) governing what constitutes an appropriate photo which is moderated before being approved.[3]

Showcasing the Body: Digitally Mediated Photos on Grindr

In choosing photos to place on their Grindr profile, the men I interviewed were bringing their bodies into 'digital being' (Thompson-Bonner 2017: 1612). The process of choosing photos was the subject of deliberation as it was the principle vehicle with which to perform sexual identity to others. As I discussed in the previous chapter, the men quickly learned the potential their muscular bodies held in capturing the attention of other men either, in the gym or in nightclubs, but also in accumulating a large following on social media. The men's use of Grindr facilitated their entry into sex work on their own terms by creating ambiguous profiles that suggested, or could be *read* by potential clients, as commercial sex availability. This reliance on other users to read one's profile to identify a more nuanced meaning was not exclusive to those advertising sex work, rather a common feature for all Grindr users. You can't explicitly say, 'I'm looking for sex' one of Blackwell's et al. (2014: 11) respondents tell them of their experience using Grindr, leaving it to the viewer to discover the real intention. While users have to learn to read photos and the text, often these can be ambiguous and contradictory (Ahlm 2017: 369). Even if that true intention is revealed, the exchange of photos using private messaging can suggest both a front- and backstage performance of online identities. My interviewees, like the respondents in Jaspal's (2017: 194) study, also played with Grindr's categories, sometimes choosing 'Latino' from the ethnicity preferences, especially when looking for work but other times clicking 'white', 'mixed' or 'other'.

The ambiguousness of users' intentions allowed my interviewees to evaluate and 'screen' the responses they received before confirming they were in fact available for sex. Just how ambiguous the choice of the photos, text and the use of emoji deployed in their profiles correlated to their financial needs at any particular time. For example, several men told a similar story where upon arrival in Dublin they had to wait for their PPS or social security card to be processed before seeking employment. This time lag and unanticipated high accommodation costs when they arrived were cited as a key entry point to their involvement in sex work.

> *Luan (27)*: The money I had went when I arrived, it went back [€3000 in funds to show immigration authorities] so I had no money and was living in a hostel so I would go on Grindr and use photos of me on the beach in my city, sometimes I would put the $ sign, but it was enough to get business, I saw a lot of guys in this time, I didn't want to do it.
>
> *Gilherme (28)*: The agency, it lied to me, they did everything in Brazil and told me I could get a place by myself for €500 [in Dublin], they lied and there is nothing I could do, I could not go home … I met guys on Grindr who contacted me, offering €60 or €80 [for sex] I was desperate and I took it … It was easy, I choose a photo from the gym, I wrote XXL, it was easy but they were bad guys I think, things weren't good for me then and they knew, now I choose the guys I meet.

The use of emoji described by Luan above had become a popular way in which men advertised there availability without inserting words like 'escort' in their profiles. It also meant that emoji could be removed and reinserted easily without changing the photo. The most recognisable emoji used was the diamond—popular because it was perceived to be only known amongst men who sold sex and their potential clients, thus remaining anonymous. In a relatively small gay community, some men were conscious of the potential stigma that being exclusively associated with sex work would have on their long-term ability to make friends, date and work in Ireland. Rafael (26) describes how many Irish gay

men didn't like Brazilians and would not meet them—'I see it on profiles [on Grindr] 'no Brazilian, no Asian' they think we have orgies and
take drugs all the time *(laughs)*, like we are the same ... Brazilians that
are escorts make that worse, we all become whores ... I would like to
meet an Irish guy and have a relationship'. The ethnic screening that
Rafael refers to is part of a wider online culture of *no*—no couples, no
hook-ups, no poz, no fem, no fat, no chems—that dominate user profiles (Tziallas 2015: 768).

The photos men like Rafael chose reflected a tension between communicating sufficient ambiguity about their online sexual motives so as
not to acquire a sex worker identity, but also being suggestive enough to
secure escort enquiries.

> *Gustavo (22)*: I choose a pic from holidays, a beach one, or a photo from
> after the gym, any photo without my shirt guys will offer money, some
> joking, time wasters some not ... if I have another normal photo – almost
> nothing! I don't like photos that are too filtered or you are looking like a
> model – guys [clients] don't like that, they want – a struggling student
> looking to make money – I think if they see you being too professional
> they are not interested, for me anyway.

Screening messages from users that are 'joking' or are 'time wasters'
is time-consuming. The men I interviewed agreed that they instinc-
tively knew real enquiries from bogus ones, with warning signs such
as demands for more photos or endless conservation about sexual preferences, with Lucas (24) describing how 'guys who want you for sex,
get to the point pretty quickly ... others are just wankers'. An una-
voidable consequence of posting photos of their muscular bodies on
Grindr is the large volume of messages that need to be filtered. Some
men, like Rodrigo (24), occasionally removed his face or body photo
entirely—'sometimes I need time to look through messages, or delete
or block, I can't do this with new messages coming in all time ... for
this I post a photo of my dog, but then even guys that like dogs message
to say 'cute dog' – ah leave me alone'. It would be incorrect to think
that Grindr is solely about performing an erotic identity; my interviews illustrate that men were involved in the performance of multiple

identities through the choice of their photos. If we return to Rafael who expressed the desire to find a relationship, we see that there is often a disjuncture between what is performed and communicated to others and the 'real' self. He describes how he changes his photo to attract different types of guys.

> If I am not looking for [sex] work I use a regular photo, like how I am to you now, the muscular guy photos get you a lot of messages but they aren't guys that I want to date, the guys I want to message are smart guys, ordinary guys and when they see this [shirtless] photo of me they think I am arrogant or stupid so I don't like to use all the time.

He continues to explain how his photos communicate a persona to potential clients that doesn't reflect his own desires and intimate needs.

> I put up photos and I am a big guy, so guys want me always to be top [sexually active] always and I do, but it is different when I want someone to date, that is not really me but it keeps it [work] separate because I can do it, but it is not what I want, when I am with someone I like, I want to be held and cuddled, I want to feel safe.

In this way, Grindr's interactive categories struggle to accommodate both the complexity of motivation that brings users online and the corporate restrictions placed upon the company that emphasise the 'dating' dimension of the app (Tziallas 2015: 763).[4]

Online, Real Time and Hybrid Space

Grindr allowed the men I interviewed traverse the city creating an interface between the online and real-time dimensions in their lives. The concept of *hybridization* recognises that the online world is no longer distinct and independent from the physical one and the role new technologies have in creating this connectedness, particularly in the online performance of sexual identities (Ryan 2016: 1714; Kitchin and Dodge 2011). Depending on the cultural context, the online

Grindr community may just offer an anonymous platform to connect with other gay men, to discuss and explore sexual identities (Valentine 2006: 379). Alternatively, it enables the online world to come alive in real time. I argue that this extra layer of online interaction over physical space facilitated and mediated interactions that would otherwise not take place. These interfaces, or hybrid spaces (De Souza e Silva 2006: 271), are utilised by my interviewees to connect the physical and the online to facilitate entry into sex work. I have identified three interface locations where this occurs regularly in the men's lives.

1. The Commute

The majority of my interviewees lived in central Dublin or within a 2-km radius of it, where they also studied English, but six men travelled to the suburbs for work by bus or tram. These 30-minute journeys were an opportunity to log onto Grindr as they travelled from the city centre, into suburbs usually less ethnically diverse. Logging on as the tram or bus moved brought the men into contact with users who would have been unable to see their profile due to the increased distance. It was also brought users into contact with men beyond the familiarity of those users within the radius of their homes and workplaces (Batiste 2013: 125–126; Ahlm 2017: 369). All six men reported meeting clients in this way, clients that represented a different cohort than would have contacted them in the city centre. Leo (25) and Joao (27) describe these encounters.

> *Leo (25)*: It is different, I travel to work and guys message me asking if I am local to them but I am nice and say 'only travelling through', sometimes the same guys talk to me and ask me to get off [the tram] at their stop to meet, it would be the third or fourth time that they suggest that they would pay, I can't remember sometime I have the diamond emoji on, sometimes not. So I meet some guys like this but I don't like – I don't know the areas and I'm always more nervous maybe it's a joke or I'm going to get beaten up or something. I have been lucky, I think these guys married, men and women, I think, I know from the houses.

Joao (27): In the city I meet guys in hotels, they are visitors for work, when on the tram people message in the area and ask if I am an escort or they message with just – €100? I have met guys this way but one time I was in his bedroom and I heard someone downstairs and I was scared – you don't know who it was or what will happen so I prefer hotels, I feel safer.

Unless a Grindr user is living in a central urban location, one that has a continual traffic of other users, travel and movement are an essential part of the app to discover others beyond one's immediate surroundings. Stempfhuber and Liegl's (2016: 66) respondents also stress this necessity for movement to keep Grindr 'working' by creating new erotic landscapes.

2. The Gym

The gym played a central role in the lives of the men I interviewed. I have discussed in the previous chapter how the gym became a platform and a showcase for the men's physically, illustrating their self-discipline and determination. Life in the gym was lived out both online and offline. Many of the photos chosen by the men in their Grindr profiles were taken at the gym. In the following chapter, I discuss how their Instagram stories are populated with videos of them working out at the gym or preparing food afterwards. Grindr allows men to communicate when they will be in the gym, as we saw with Rafael (26) in Chapter 2, encouraging men to 'come up and say hello'. The men also receive messages from other users, telling them that had seen them in the gym and was it OK to come and talk with them. These interactions provide clients with a way of 'knowing' the men they meet for sex. Other messages are more direct requests for sexual services. Bruno (21) offers an example of this type of request, similar to what other men I interviewed have also received.

Bruno (21): I get a lot of messages about the gym, about working out, exercises and diets, guys are looking for advice, sometimes they ask can they work out with me … I have done that for €50 and there is no sex,

we work out and it is easy, they [clients] decide what we do and sometimes they ask me to wear some shorts or a t-shirt that they have seen me
in the gym in … I have a Superman t-shirt, you know? It is the logo in
red, this guy asks me to wear that and it is cool … Sometimes guys ask to
massage me after the gym, this is funny because I wrote massage on my
other profile [PlanetRomeo] but I said I would do it, but I can't *(laughs)*
and now they want to do it, it's strange, no?

It is unsurprising given Bruno's experience that four of the men I interviewed now work as personal trainers. The interface between gym and
sex work has allowed these men to recast their online personas promoting the cultivation of the body in a health and fitness frame, rather than
an exclusively erotic one. It also legitimatises the construction of their
Grindr and Instagram profiles which showcase their bodies for a professional purpose, however suggestive the material. As personal trainers,
their bodies symbolise the 'embodied labour' of health and fitness clubs,
creating a consumer desire amongst the membership to train harder to
achieve their goals (Frew and McGillivray 2005: 171). However, rather
than acting as inspiration, the bodies of personal training staff often act
more as a mirror to remind the membership of their own undisciplined
bodies.

3. Club Nights

Dublin's gay scene has continued to evolve in tandem with the city,
responding to economic boom and bust, migration and a demand for
more diverse club nights. The oldest and traditional bar and club, *The
George,* have recently seen competition from a range of weekly and
monthly club nights operating from different venues. Here, there is a
rejection of commercial pop music in favour of house, in an atmos-
phere that seeks to replicate circuit styles clubs—or parties—popular
in Barcelona and Ibiza. These clubs have offered theme nights complete
with go-go dancers and theatre. It is within this environment that digital identities come alive in real time. Four men I interviewed found
work here, as both dancers and as a door host. Erick (22), a Venezuelan
student, had previously worked in a straight city centre club working

as a server on weekly Spanish and Brazilian nights, an experience he described as the 'worst of his life', being forced to be shirtless wearing cut-off jeans while being subject to more harassment than his female colleagues.

> It gets worse the later it gets and the more they [customers] drink, you have people touching you, they grab … your ass, your cock, they squeeze your nipples and you have to be polite because it's all joking … I hate it, I really it hate and it's only €12 an hour.

Experiences like Erick's reveal that whatever satisfaction male sex workers gained in having their bodies admired and gaze upon, it was highly dependent on the level of control the men were able to exercise over the encounters. Scull's (2013: 571) study of male strippers also revealed men having their genitals grabbed and being scratched, bitten and left bleeding by ardent female patrons. Moving to work in the gay club night as a dancer, although less frequent, was a more positive experience that, in turn, benefited Erick's sex work. However, the sexual harassment wasn't over, as Erick explains –

> I got the job as a dancer which is funny because I can't really dance, not all Latin men can dance you know? It was more moving than dancing, but I had to meet the guy that runs the club before and it was horrible, really, I don't want to talk about it, he was so sleazy, horrible, but when I got the job, I loved it, good people, you were on a stage so people look at you but nobody touched you … On Grindr a lot of people would message and say – oh I know you – It was good for [sex] work too, guys knew you and that you were not going to be some crazy bitch *(laughs)*.

Disposable Bodies? Converting Physical Capital

The men's stories clearly show the successful conversion of their physical capital into economic opportunities in sex work, personal training and waiting staff. It has opened social opportunities for them to join a more vibrant club scene where some acquired work. These conversions do, however I argue, go beyond physical capital. Catherine Hakim's (2010) concept of *erotic capital*, although much derided by feminist scholarship, provides some useful applications to the men's lives. It is clear when analysing these stories, the men in my study see sex work as neither a career, nor a job (although there are references to work) rather a *resource* to be drawn down at times when it was most needed. I argue that we need to understand male sex work as less about *career* as it is shown to be discontinuous, defying simplistic 'entry and exit' models. As I argue later in this chapter, most men see sex work as a resource that can be utilised over a longer time period, should the market allow them to do so. Hakim (2010: 500–501) identities her six (or seven) elements of erotic capital. The culturally contingent concept of beauty and sexual attractiveness extended across the men's lives. I discussed in Chapter 2, where men commonly spoke of how they were 'considered more attractive here than at home'. A racialisation and fetishisation of specific bodily characteristics by Irish gay culture had secured a space for those bestowed with them to accrue benefits across a range of social locations. Hakim further identifies a social dimension, charm and grace, along with liveliness, style and presentation and sexuality itself. Hakim (2010: 501) describes erotic capital as 'a combination of aesthetic, visual, physical, social and sexual attractiveness to other members of your society'. While Hakim's analysis is largely of heterosexual relationships, her view that women have greater levels of erotic capital because they work harder on presentation and the performance of sexuality draws parallels with the experience of gay men, particularly the stories of those told in this book. Particularly when Hakim (2010: 506) identifies the role that erotic capital plays in the lives of those with diminished capital in other areas, including 'young people, ethnic and cultural minorities, and working class groups'. Hakim argues that patriarchal society's denigration of erotic capital is most obvious in the stigmatisation of female sex workers. By contrast within marriage and mate selection, beauty, along with educational credentials, are identified by Hakim (2000: 162) as influential.

The conversion of the physical and erotic capital accrued by my interviewees was at time challenging. There were differing levels of commitment to remaining in Ireland, with eight men acknowledging their desire to stay. They speculated on how to achieve this, mostly through enrolment in a recognised third-level educational institution, or pursuing a European passport through relatives in Portugal and Italy. It was their precarious lives that made it more difficult to form relationships with other Dublin residents—who felt that their stay in the city would be temporary.

> *Lucas (24)*: Meeting guys is not easy for me, especially Irish, they think we [Brazilians] are here for nine months or a year so we are just something for fun [sex], that's all they want. They all want fit guys but when they had sex with you they are gone.

This view that the time spent developing their bodies was actually a disadvantage in meeting men that they sought relationships with was shared by many. The interviewees felt that they were often unfairly stereotyped as brainless party boys, with a proclivity for G—the most popular drug in the gay community. Rafael (26) describes his last dating experience.

> I was with this guy, I liked him, he was Irish and we dated for four months maybe, five and it was good … after two months I knew that he knew all my friends and I knew no one, none of his friends, I was like – what is this? He thinks I'm stupid? He is embarrassed of me? He thinks I am too young and his dentist friends will be all … you know. I was really sad about it, I felt like shit. He was so nice and good to me but he was afraid of these people, his friends.

Thiago (21) also spoke similarly of his experience dating an Irish guy in his thirties who ended their relationship by telling him that an older Irish guy dating a younger Brazilian was 'too much of cliché'. Thiago was adamant it would have been different if he was French or Spanish national and that he was 'thrown away' by his boyfriend. Most interviewees spoke similarly about how, although they were desired and coveted, their bodies were also disposable. In this regard, their stories of dating and sex work were remarkable similar, often describing how they were picked by guys who had no interest in any conversation with them, either before or after sex. 'It's the same [for dating & sex work] when they cum, they want you to go away so fast' Rafael (26) recalling an experience with a man who he had an ambiguous causal relationship with that involved occasional payments to him. He describes—'I was on my knees looking for my socks [after sex] and he was standing over me saying 'do you really need them?' and I thought it is February you asshole, yea, I need my socks'. Rafael suffers what Bauman (2003: 65) describes, as 'termination on demand', an unfortunate consequence of when sex moves into the digital world. In this world, dating resembles browsing through a catalogue with 'no obligation to buy' ensuring that human connectedness will increasing be more frequent and shallow (p. 62).

Sex, Money and Intimacy

In sex work encounters, there was a law of diminishing returns, where the significant numbers of young Brazilian and Venezuelan men on dating apps reduced their perceived exoticness, which was once the key to their success. This resulted in clients' willingness to negotiate and haggle over prices. It was also the consequence of deploying a transient sex work identity online, communicating to viewers that they could be available to you for sex, at the right price. That price is, however, open to negotiation. Sometimes, there was not cash price but the payment of goods or services. This occurred in three of the men's stories where a lump sum was paid to ensure continuing access, sexual and companionship, although the terms seemed nebulous and were far from contractual.

> *Joao (27)*: I ask for €150 always, but [clients] sometimes say – I only want this or that or something like I'm not old so here's €50 – really? Or sometimes they are want it free … it is always a really bad sign, a warning for something bad later.
>
> *Renzo (23)*: When I first came here I was dating this guy, well was it dating? We were getting to know each other and he paid for my English course, I remember it was really soon and there was no talk about

anything, if it meant anything, he just did it and I learned that you don't ask for things, they are given ... It was a lot of money, it was a big deal for me. We lost contact but met again, my mother was not well, she was having a hysterectomy and he paid for my ticket home, it was so generous to get so little in return.

Joao's suspicion of potential clients who haggle over the price is shared in other accounts from male sex workers' online (e.g. McClean 2013: 10), where those in a financial position to refuse such clients, do so. This movement of sex work beyond the traditional exchange of money for sex in Renzo's account is a significant feature of all the stories in this book. Although these exchanges took place, online identities had facilitated a growing ambiguity around the boundaries of sexual encounters and the levels of intimacy within them. These relationships could be characterised as 'friends with benefits' or 'fuck buddies' where an exchange occurred of economic benefits for sexual and intimate companionship. This concept is not new. The concept of the 'kept-boy' had been categorised in the scientific literature on male prostitution in the 1970s, representing the face of 'private' as opposed to public or street prostitution (Scott 2003: 189). Hall's (2007: 467) ethnographic study in Prague also explored this relationship between a younger Czech and an older, wealthy German businessman. While both expressed love for each other, the boundaries of their sexual fidelity were unclear, leading to feelings of jealously, while the younger man felt excluded from his boyfriend's circle of close friends, amid gossip that he had previously been a sex worker. This scenario was very similar to that recalled by Rafael's relationship in the previous section.

The ways in which men can be compensated for either sex, companionship or online content have become increasingly diverse, and I return to discuss some of these platforms, like Amazon Wish List and OnlyFans, in Chapter 4. Renzo's quote about receiving free flights home also highlights the role of intimacy within sex work encounters. Walby's (2012: 133) interviews with male sex workers reveal varying degrees of intimacy with clients, particularly those they have met on a number of occasions. These stories tell of clients' emotional demands to be held and touched as opposed to other forms of sexual activity. The escorts tell of encounters with clients where they are enjoying sex, where there is no faking and no performance of a feigned intimacy. Intimacy becomes recast in these sexual encounters beyond concepts of monogamy, love and long-term commitment (p. 115). There is evidence in my interviews of a desire for intimacy and an emotional contact motivating some clients when they arranged sex worker dates. I say this tentatively because this book does not draw upon the perspective of clients and their diverse motivations to seek paid sex, but clients who booked sex workers more than once, did often enter into encounters that were more intimate. Consider Rodrigo's story, one reflected in other accounts.

> One of my first clients was an older guy … a big guy who was very emotional … I had taken my clothes off and he was crying and I'm not sure what's happening, he was just saying that I was beautiful, again and again and we did not do much, he looked at me for ages … It was me, or not maybe, for him maybe I was him much younger and that made him feel sad but he always treated me like I was this God to him

Rodrigo continues by telling the story of another client who he met on a number of occasions:

> We did have sex once but then he messaged me to go for coffee, it was around 3pm, I was not sure about his [family] situation, he wanted to talk, I never understood it, it is easy for me, the best but sometimes it is stranger than sex, you know? What does he want from? Advice?
> *(Paul - interviewer)*: So he paid you in full for those coffee dates?
> *Rodrigo (24)*: He did, he paid me €150 each time. I was as surprised as you. I think there is some strange therapy thing here, sometimes during sex they say it too – like 'I could never be this free with an Irish guy' like they are exploring sex or something?

There are similar accounts given by male sex workers in their experiences with clients who are married or uncomfortable with their sexuality and where escorts can become a source of comfort in such situations (Parsons et al. 2007: 233). They are also similar to relationships between

regular male clients and female sex workers who told of receiving emotional support and friendship from the women they met over a pro-
longed period of time (Sanders 2008: 409–410). These encounters with
clients were identified by my interviewees as the most favourable; they
had met them before, they had paid as agreed, and they felt comfortable with them. This was often in sharp contrast to first time encounters with clients, where the men almost unanimously, sought to remain
in control of the meeting. This was achieved through the construction
of their profile and in initial conversations with potential clients. They
overwhelming choose the category—top—indicating they were solely
sexually active, irrespective of whether they were or not. The initial conversations conveyed that their natural preference was to be dominant in
the sexual encounter, and this enabled them to maintain the focus on
their own bodies rather than their clients, a useful strategy with those
they found less attractive. In these encounters, the traditional gaze on
the sex worker's body is subverted as explained here by Thiago.

> I do enjoy the sex but only when I am in control of what is happening,
> this is easier with older or fat guys who don't want it about their bodies,
> they want it about mine so I love that … watching them enjoy my body
> and I get paid, it's easy for me …

It illustrates that the possession of physical capital also is embedded
within power relations, where those who possess it, use it to symbol-
ically dominate those that do not (Bourdieu 1984). This also creates
what Boden (2007: 130) describes as a 'subcultural prestige' within
the gay community where their youth, beauty and muscular bodies
transform them into the most desirable men available. The experience
of being the object of such attention and sexual desire proved to be
almost addictive to some male escorts who returned to work after ini-
tially deciding to leave sex work (Parsons et al. 2007: 235). While the
excitement of being desired is identified by my interviewees as being
important, so is the actually physical pleasure of client sexual encounters. A majority of the men reported that they had a heightened interest in sex and continued to have a large number of partners, even at

times they were not engaged in sex work, in line with previous studies (Vanwesenbeeck 2012).

Touring

A majority of the men I interviewed were involved in touring—or travelling to other cities to for sex work, a common practice identified in sex work studies (e.g. Sanders et al. 2018: 63). Again, there were many different experiences. For some, it was a pit stop to earn money before continuing to travel but for others sex work was again, a resource which they drew upon as they travelled abroad to fund the trip. Decisions about which cities to visit were made on economic criteria—how much clients were prepared to pay and also their perceived sexual desirability in those cities. Zurich and Vienna were the overwhelming favourite destinations for the men I interviewed to visit. The men used profiles on both Grindr and a profile on the escort site, rentmen.eu when they travelled.

> *Renzo (23)*: A friend suggested Zurich to me, I had no idea about it, I was told it was more expensive than Dublin but that people earned a lot more money there … it was really nice to visit but not to stay longer, I worked there for a week and it really is great, even with hotel and plane, you do very well … You have to understand that it is like Grindr for everyone, the new person gets all the messages, there are only some people in Dublin and then the visitors but in Zurich when you visit you are the new face, I met two or three guys a day when I was there, on some trips I made over €3000.
>
> *Joao (27)*: It was good for me to go [Vienna] it is better, in Dublin you can wait and wait for work but here when you go you just work every day and try to see many guys, it is better for me, I feel that I am a stranger there, my photos what I write I don't care there – this is me, I am working now come get me! *(laughs)* I like that it is apart from my friends and life in Dublin … Last year I went [Vienna] before going to the Circuit party in Barcelona so I could pay for the tickets and have a good holiday.

Barcelona's Circuit party is an eleven-day gay dance festival held in August. Spread over different venues in the city, it has become synonymous with the display of muscular bodies, drug use and sexual excess. It was identified, by my interviewees, as one of the social highlights of their year, for which they trained harder in the gym in the preceding months to be in the best physical shape. The relationship between Circuit parties, sexual inhibition and drug use has been explored in both the USA (O'Byrne and Holmes 2011) and Europe (Gaissad 2013). Other interviewees told me how they financed longer trips abroad through sex work. Victor (25) travelled to Thailand last year and decided to work for a week in Singapore before his holiday.

> I checked online and to find somewhere that would be good to work, Singapore is expensive and you need somewhere OK and nice and clean if you are working and want guys to come but it was good for me to go … I think that the white guys won't have sex with the Asian guys so you have these Asian guys with money that want white guys – or guys like me – but they can't get them so there is a lot of guys who want to meet up, I worked every day and people give tips and are polite

Coercion

The men reported no accounts of physical assault or acts of violence against them by clients in the course of their work. They attributed this to both their physical size, often much larger than their clients, and how they negotiated the initial encounters. However, there were numerous accounts of coercion perpetrated against them that sought to exploit their precarious position in the state. The most serious of which was a client known to many of my interviewees, who purported to be working for the Irish immigration service. The men's stories were remarkably similar telling how he had arranged to meet them, and then refusing to pay, he threatened them with deportation.

> *Gilherme (28)*: I never knew if it was true but I was scared, maybe because in my country you do not want trouble with the police so I let him walk

away … friends told me this guy was well known and it was not a secret and he did work for immigration.

Erick (22): We all knew him, I remember my friends writing in a WhatsApp group warning us to avoid him … it was hard, he got guys in the office building and contacted us on Grindr threatening us with all things.

The lack of availability of good quality and affordable housing also made the men's lives more precarious, particularly upon their arrival in Dublin. Often living with a host family or a hostel for a number of months, pressure mounted to secure accommodation. The options were limited. Stories revealed early months of living in shared rooms with six other men in houses accommodating up to twelve people. Others fared relatively better sharing a room in an apartment, but few had a private room in which to accommodate clients, the revenue from which could only ensure them an escape to a better standard of accommodation. Lucas (24) told of his attempts to rent a room in a home owner's house from an advertisement he saw on Grindr, which ended badly.

> I knew it was a bad idea but I was in a bad place and I did it, it was awful from the start, he [the owner] would make jokes about me cleaning the house in my underwear and then in my room I saw things that moved and I knew he was there … one night he approached me for sex, it was just easier to have sex with him than say no, so I did … two weeks later I brought someone home [for sex] and he heard us and the next day he kicked me out with nothing, no notice, just get out now

Often unable to provide landlords with work references and bank account statements, men were reliant on existing networks with their own communities alerting them to apartment vacancies. The men were living in a range of different accommodation, some sharing a two-bed-room apartment and receiving in-calls, others remaining in shared accommodation and doing out-calls, mostly to hotels. Gustavo (22) describes his current apartment, a modern two bedroom apartment in the city centre which he shares with another sex worker that was secured with fake work references, common amongst the men I interviewed.

It has a small balcony that overlooks the gate entrance which Gustavo checks to see whether the client enters alone. There are two bedrooms, the larger one he shares with his flatmate, and the smaller one where they both use to see clients. It is sparse; a double bed covered in a white sheet with no pillows and no duvet. A small bedside table has wet wipes, lubricant and poppers. It is here that I interview Gustavo, sitting on the bed, after which I pay him our agreed €50 and leave. He describes living here.

> This place I share with a friend, he had it first, it is a really good place in a good location and it is big enough [complex] to be not noticed by anyone. My flatmate is a little crazy that's the only problem, he had an injury and was not at the gym and now he is using steroids and he is getting huge but he gets angry and shouts a lot – sometimes I hear shouting in the work room and I'm like – is he killing them? *(laughs)* They must like it because he does better than me.

Being online necessitated dealing with a large volume of messages. This resulted in the interviewees either refusing offers of sex, sex for money or leaving a large number of messages unanswered leading to abusive messages. Sometimes this abuse was racial, frequently telling the men to 'go home' or physical, where they were told they were ugly or conceited or messages of general profanity. These messages did not pose any real concern to my interviewees, who saw it as an everyday part of digital life. However, there were two examples of where this abuse became more problematic. Leo (25) describes how after two conversations on Grindr, he declined an offer to meet a client only to subsequently meet him in a bar the following week. He said 'oh you think you are all that don't you? You are nothing but a whore'—Leo tells me as they came face to face in a crowded bar. He described the man expression—'he was really angry, I didn't remember him and he knew that, I talk to a lot of people, but I remembered his face, it was so angry, like he really hated me'. The second example of online abuse, which almost all the interviewees reported, was that of *catfish*—or people who steal photos and impersonate you online (Drouin et al. 2016). There were different experiences of being catfished, most of which were benign. Renzo (23) describes:

> There are photos of me everywhere I think, I see on different sites and guys message and tell me that they were talking to me for six months and I say – sorry – that wasn't me but these guys are stupid, it is easy to test and see if it [profile] is for real or not and the guys that do this, it is so sad that I cannot get angry for it, I think these are old, fat men at home wanking asking men for photos and sending mine, it is really sad.

The majority of interviewees felt resigned about the likelihood of their photos or identity being stolen by others believing it was an avoidable consequence of socialising online, and believing like Renzo above, users have to use 'checks' to screen authenticity, like connecting to Instagram or exchanging phone numbers for WhatsApp. This concern about the misrepresentation of personal information and the fear of having one's own identity and photographs stolen by others was a fear that generated mistrust and was shared by users of Grindr (Corriero and Tong 2016: 133; Tziallas 2015: 769; Sanders et al. 2018: 109). The geolocative features of Grindr and the heightened expectation users have of connecting with people in real time did not mitigate their fear of deception and misrepresentation. Not all catfish experiences were harmless. Bruno (21) explained how he was alerted by friends to a fake profile using his photos on Grindr that was asking people to engage in unsafe sex. 'I saw the profile once, a friend had took a photo of it and it said that I was HIV positive which is a lie … they reported it but nothing happened'. Bruno had no idea who the person was, but suspected it was someone who he had rejected sexually who now had embarked upon this campaign to damage his reputation.

GHB

While the use of steroids was uncommon, just two interviewees admitting usage throughout their lives, the use of the drug G (GHB) was commonplace. GHB, or gamma hydroxybutyrate, is a depressive agent which, given in the right dosage, creates a euphoric high that stimulates the libido (Nicholson and Balster 2001). My interviewees reported using GHB with their friends, during sex and also with their clients. Despite their knowledge of unpleasant and potentially dangerous side effects amongst their friends, these did not dampen their enthusiasm for the drug, of which they felt competent to use. 'Everyone has a G story' Gustavo (22) tells me, recalling times when his friends had passed out from the drug at home, in clubs and on public transport. 'We were going to the centre on the bus from a party somewhere outside and my friend took too much, or thinks it is not working and he takes another spoon, but was asleep on the bus, unconscious and we could not wake him … we went to the bus station and carried him off, we told the driver he was drunk …'. Luan (27) also had similar stories of the drug, of novice users' projectile vomiting from an incorrect dosage to couples starting to have sex on the floor of their apartment while they had guests over dinner. Increased satisfaction was a key motivator for the use of G by my interviewees. This desire also blurred the boundaries between their recreational sex and sex work, a situation which often saw clients brought into the men's personal lives. More than half of the interviewees admitted to having sex with a client while on G, or another drug, while seven men told of having invited clients or potential clients to house sex parties. The drug, along with mephedrone and crystal methamphetamine or Tina, has been identified as more prevalent amongst sexually active gay men and also constitutes what has been described as *chemsex* (Bourne et al. 2015: 565). The Bourne et al. (2015) study describes the use of these drugs during sex parties, usually held in private homes over a long period of time; this reference by respondents to 'chemsex marathons' does correspond to Rafael (26) description below.

> *Gilherme (28)*: I don't do drugs with guys [clients] that often, but if they offer G, I will because I know it and I have taken it many times, it is good with clients that you don't like [physically] because it makes you so horny but it is all over in an hour and you can get to your job or do things.
> *Rafael (26)*: I take it too much I think, sometimes alone if I am bored and in my house but more with friends or at a party … we take it at

a party [club] and then go to a house of my friend and it goes on and on … sometimes it is a little crazy because we are on Grindr asking guys to come to and if they have G or something I'm saying – please come, please come … there is trouble sometimes with neighbours because there is much noise, and coming and going, sometimes a guy [client] who I have met will ask to come and it is ok for me … I will have sex with that [points to a waste paper bin] when I'm on G, it does not matter to me

Race (2015b: 267) has also examined how Grindr users advertise for others to join extended chemsex sessions, while taking a combination of crystal methamphetamine, GHB and Viagra. These sessions are motivated by sex, but are punctuated by chill out periods, chatting and going online to make contact with others, usually in private homes. While previous research has suggested differing motivations for taking GHB, like relaxation for example (McDowell 2000), my interviewees were overwhelming using it within a sexual context. Palamar and Halkitis' (2006: 26) sample of gay male users similarly found that all had reported that it had increased their desire for sex, lowered their inhibitions and increased the prospects of greater sexual promiscuity. They further reported that the preference for GHB, as opposed to other drugs, was that the recovery time from the effects were shorter. This time motivation is reflected in Gilherme's quote above, in which he suggests it is more suitable for male sex workers by increasing desire but enabling workers to resume their lives with little side effects afterwards. All my interviewees agreed that the use of GHB did not impair their ability to conduct safer sex with their clients on a one-to-one basis, although many did become more circumspect about describing occasions of unsafe sex during private parties with their friends and other guests.

Exiting Sex Work—The Long Goodbye

Policy makers throughout the European Union have embraced the concept of 'exiting' as a key, and often sole, strategy in the governance of prostitution, moving women into regular employment (Scoular and

O'Neill 2007: 767). These exit strategies, almost exclusively directed towards women, often ignore the complexities of the social exclusion experienced by sex workers which make these transitions unrealistic for many. Academic research has followed suit, with a greater interest in exploring exit, rather than entry to sex work (Cusick et al. 2011: 146). I have cast doubt on the usefulness of exit models from prostitution when describing the lives of my interviewees in this chapter. Like Cusick et al. (2011: 147) argue, exit is not one event, but a sequence of events. Rather, I have suggested that sex work exists in their lives as neither a profession nor a source of activism, but rather a resource with which they have drawn upon throughout their adult lives. This lack of involvement within sex work activism has also been identified in recent surveys with only a minority of those involved (Sanders et al. 2018: 45). The motivations that brought them to Ireland were diverse and while my interviewees' lives remain precarious in terms of career and migration status, the likelihood of the men continuing to draw upon sex work remains high. Some fear there is a little to return home to in either Venezuela or Brazil, due to economic or family reasons, with Erick (22) describing how his family 'are happy that I am here and that I am safe … there is nothing in my country [Venezuela] for me or my family, it is breaking down and I'm so scared for them'. Joao (27) told of his commitment to work in Ireland as a personal trainer and that he had 'no home in my country [Brazil] my mother has moved from my city with her new husband, so my house is gone, my room is gone'. For others, the income from sex work is contributing not just to everyday living, but to a specific purpose in their lives. For Victor, whose grandfather is Italian, his extra money from sex work will fund his living costs when he moves to Italy, a necessity when applying for his new passport. Renzo's (23) plans are even more ambitious—as he is saving to pay for flight school in the USA to secure his pilot's licence—which he suggests will take 'another five years'. I discuss Renzo's use of social media to generate income in more detail in the next chapter.

Unlike so much of the literature on male sex work in Ireland, there is no evidence that this income is exclusively funding problematic drug use. However, as we saw in this chapter, the men do spend income on drugs like GHB, a habit they see as less detrimental to their health, than the copious amounts of alcohol consumed by other gay men in bars and clubs every week. A closer comparison to the earlier body of research on male sex work in Ireland would be the impact of homelessness. While none of the men I interviewed described themselves as homeless, a number did tell stories of moving from couch to couch, staying at friend's houses, which were often already overcrowded. Income from sex work played a vital role for men in this situation to save for deposits or secure a shared room in a house.

The law governing prostitution in Ireland changed in 2017. The Criminal Law (Sexual Offences) Act makes the purchase of sex illegal and continues to criminalise sex workers who work in pairs under brothel keeping laws (Ryan and Ward 2017). At the time of my interviews, this topic was being contentiously debated in the parliamentary committees and on television and radio current affairs programmes. Although these debates exclusively focused on female sex workers, the men I interviewed had little or no knowledge of the law, nor would any change in the law influence their decision to stop selling sex. When I told the men of the impending legal change, several expressed confusion about how the sex purchase ban would work in practice. Leo (25), for example, wondered 'do [the police] they come into your bedroom … how would that happen? They break the door of your bedroom and look at the sex that you are having, if there is money? How would that work?' Renzo (23) similarly wondered if the law was for the transfer of cash only and whether the flight home he received from a client would be included—'Who would decide? I don't understand how they would know how my flight or my English classes were paid by someone that is not me but also how would they know what I did so they would pay? Do you understand?' The men are right to question the enforcement of the law. The Police Service of Northern Ireland (PSNI) cast doubt on whether the law could be enforced to investigate consensual commercial sex given scarce police resources in a study undertaken prior to the introduction of a similar law in Northern Ireland (Huschke et al. 2014).

Conclusion

This chapter has explored how Grindr is a platform used by the men in this study to display their bodies, to accrue physical and erotic capital and deploy and convert that capital into economic opportunities. It has traced the evolution of casual sexual encounters amongst men, from public space to cinemas and saunas into the digital era where identities are constructed and performed online that seek to connect with others. These online mobile identities travel with the user, opening new possibilities of connection in diverse neighbourhoods and social environments of the city, where they map onto the existing physical space becoming a hybrid of online and real-time interaction. This chapter explored different interfaces where this occurred—in their commute, the gym and in clubs—to create new opportunities for sex, dating and sex work.

The ease with which photos and profile text can be changed facilitated the men in my study to tailor their identities to specific audiences at specific times. The judicious use of photos showcasing their bodies communicated the potential for sex work, in addition to the use of particular emoji's that confirmed that availability to the potential clients that read them. These online profiles travelled abroad, as the men in this study travelled to cities like Zurich and Vienna for sex work 'tours' or were used to generate income that permitted further travel. I argued that sex work existed in the men's lives as a *resource* which could be drawn down in situations where income needed to be generated quickly and often for a specific purpose. Grindr is used to create these possibilities, in ways that are opportunistic and transient given the context. The stories that contributed to this chapter are diverse. Men had different educational background and plans to pursue careers either in Ireland or in Venezuela or Brazil. Their use of sex work was drawn upon to solve urgent short-term problems like housing, but also contributed to the realisation of long-term dreams. It wasn't a resource that came without risk or exploitation. While avoiding the prospect of physical assault, their precarious migration and work situations left them vulnerable to other forms exploitation as they struggled to secure housing and work.

Notes

1. Options include—**Body type**: do not show, toned, average, large, muscular, slim, stocky; **Ethnicity**: do not show, Asian, Black, Latino, Middle Eastern, Mixed, Native American, White, South Asian, other; **Position**: do not show, top, vers top, versatile, vers bottom, bottom; **Tribe**: bear, clean cut, daddy, discreet, geek, jock, leather, otter, poz, rugged, trans, twink; **Relationship Status**: do not show, committed, dating, engaged, exclusive, married, open relationship, partnered, single; **I'm Looking for**: chat, dates, friends, networking, relationships, right now.
2. Grindr's announcement that had shared users' HIV status with third parties in 2018 without permission created controversy for the company who argued that sharing was 'standard practice' in the industry.
3. https://www.grindr.com/profile-guidelines.
4. The interactive categories are—chat, dates, networking, friends, relationship and right now.

References

Ahlm, J. (2017). Respectable promiscuity: Digital cruising in an era of queer liberalism. *Sexualities, 20*(3), 364–379.

Batiste, D. P. (2013). '0 Feet Away': The queer cartography of French gay men's geo-social media use. *Anthropological Journal of European Cultures, 22*(2), 111–132.

Bauman, Z. (2003). *Liquid love: On the frailty of human bonds'.* Cambridge: Polity Press.

Bérubé, A. (2003). The history of gay bathhouses. *Journal of Homosexuality, 44*(3–4), 33–53.

Binson, D., Pollack, L. M., & Woods, W. J. (2010). HIV transmission risk at a gay bathhouse. *Journal of Sex Research, 47*(6), 580–588.

Blackwell, C., Birnholtz, J., & Abbott, C. (2014). Seeing and being seen: Co-situation and impression formation using Grindr, a location-aware gay dating app. *New Media & Society, 17*(7), 1117–1136.

Boden, D. M. (2007). Alienation of sexuality in male erotic dancing. *Journal of Homosexuality, 53*(1–2), 129–252.

Bourdieu, P. (1984). *Distinction: A social critique of the judgement of taste.* London: Routledge.

Bourne, A., Reid, D., Hickson, F., Torres-Reuda, S., & Weatherburn, P. (2015). Illict drug use in sexual settings ('chemsex') and HIV/STI transmission risk behaviour among gay men in South London: Findings from a qualitative study. *Sex Transm Infect, 91,* 564–568.

Brubaker, J. R., Ananny, M., & Crawford, K. (2016). Departing glances: A sociotechnical account of 'leaving' Grindr. *New Media and Society, 18*(3), 376–390.

Burrell, E. R., Pines, H. A., Robbie, E., Coleman, L., Murphy, R. D., Hess, K. L., et al. (2012). Use of location-based social networking application Grindr as a recruitment tool in rectal microbicide development research. *AIDS and Behavior, 16*(7), 1816–1820.

Chauncey, G. (1994). *Gay New York: Gender, urban culture and the making of the gay male world, 1840–1940.* New York: Basic Books.

Corriero, E. F., & Tong, S. T. (2016). Managing uncertainty in mobile dating applications: Goals, concerns of use and information seeking in Grindr. *Mobile Media & Communication, 4*(1), 121–141.

Cusick, L., Brooks-Gordon, B., Campbell, R., & Edgar, F. (2011). 'Exiting' drug use and sex work: Career paths, interventions and government strategy targets. *Drugs, Education, Prevention and Policy, 18*(2), 145–156.

Delph, E. W. (1978). *The silent community: Public homosexual encounters.* Beverly Hills: Sage.

De Souza e Silva, A. (2006). Mobile technologies as interfaces of hybrid spaces. *Space and Culture, 9*(3), 261–278.

Drouin, M., Miller, D., Welhle, S., & Hernandez, E. (2016). Why do people lie online? "Because everyone lies on the internet". *Computers in Human Behaviour, 64,* 134–142.

Edwards, T. (1994). *Erotics & politics: Gay male sexuality, masculinity and feminism.* London: Routledge.

Frew, M., & McGillivray, D. (2005). Health clubs and body politics: Aesthetics and the quest for physical capital. *Leisure Studies, 24*(2), 161–175.

Gaissad, L. (2013). Expending ourselves at 'La Demence'? Gay party circuit from consumption to consummation. *Ethnologie Francaise, 43,* 409–416.

Hakim, C. (2000). *Work-lifestyles choices in the 21st century: Preference theory.* Oxford: Oxford University Press.

Hakim, C. (2010). Erotic capital. *European Sociological Review, 26*(5), 499–518.

Hall, T. M. (2007). Rent-boys, barflies and kept men: Men involved in sex with men for compensation in Prague. *Sexualities, 10*(4), 457–472.

Holmes, D., O'Byrne, P., & Gastaldo, D. (2007). Setting the space for sex: Architecture, desire and health issues in gay bathhouses. *International Journal of Nursing Studies, 44*, 273–284.

Humphreys, L. (1970). *Tearoom trade: Impersonal sex in public places.* Piscataway: Transaction Publishers.

Huschke, D. S., Shirlow, P. P., Schubotz, D. D., Ward, D. E., Probst, B. A., Ursula, & Ní Dhónaill, D. (2014). *Research into prostitution in Northern Ireland.* Belfast: Department of Justice, Northern Ireland.

Jaspal, R. (2017). Gay men's construction and management of identity on Grindr. *Sexuality and Culture, 21,* 187–2014.

Kitchin, R., & Dodge, M. (2011). *Code/Space: Software and everyday life.* Cambridge: MIT Press.

Lee, J. A. (1976). Forbidden colors of love: Patterns of gay love and gay liberation. *Journal of Homosexuality, 1*(4), 401–418.

Lee-Gonyea, J. A., Castle, T., & Gonyea, N. E. (2009). Laid to order: Male escorts advertising on the internet. *Deviant Behaviour, 30,* 321–348.

Lenza, M. (2004). 'Controversies surrounding Laud Humphreys' tearoom trade: An unsettling example of politics and power in methodological critiques. *International Journal of Sociology and Social Policy, 24*(3/4), 20–31.

Light, B., Fletcher, G., & Adam, A. (2008). Gay men, Gaydar and the commodification of difference. *Information, Technology & People, 21*(3), 300–314.

McClean, A. (2013). 'You can do it from your sofa': The increasing popularity of the internet as a working site among male sex workers in Melbourne. *Journal of Sociology, 51*(4), 1–16.

McDowell, D. (2000). Gay men, lesbians and substances of abuse and the 'club and circuit party scene': What clinicians should know. *Journal of Gay and Lesbian Psychotherapy, 3*(3–4), 37–57.

Nicholson, K. L. & Balster, R. L. (2001). GHB: A new and novel drug of abuse. *Drug and Alcohol Dependence, 63*(1), 1–22.

O'Byrne, P., & Holmes, D. (2011). Desire, drug use and unsafe sex: A qualitative examination of gay men who attend circuit parties. *Culture, Health and Sexuality, 13*(1), 1–13.

Palamar, J. J., & Halkitis, P. N. (2006). A qualitative analysis of GHB use among gay men: Reasons for use despite potential adverse outcomes. *International Journal of Drug Policy, 17,* 23–28.

Parsons, J. T., Koken, J. A., & Bimbi, D. S. (2004). The use of the internet by gay and bisexual male escorts: Sex workers as sex educators. *Aids Care, 16*(8), 1021–1035.

Parsons, J. T., Koken, J. A., & Bimbi, D. S. (2007). Looking beyond HIV: Eliciting individual and community needs of male internet escorts. *Journal of Homosexuality, 53*(1–2), 219–240.

Pruitt, M. V. (2005). Online boys: Mal-for-male internet escorts. *Sociological Focus, 38*(3), 189–203.

Race, K. (2015a). Speculative pragmatism and intimate arrangements: Online hook up devices in gay life. *Culture, Health and Sexuality, 17*(4), 496–511.

Race, K. (2015b). Party and play: Online hook-up devices and the emergence of PNP practices among gay men. *Sexualities, 18*(3), 253–275.

Reisen, C. A., Iracheta, M. A., Zea, M. C., Bianchi, F. T., & Poppen, P. J. (2010). Sex in public and private settings among Latino MSM. *Aids Care, 22*(6), 697–704.

Rice, E. I., Holloway, H., Winetrobe, H., Rhoades, A., Barman-Adhikari, J., Gibbs, A., et al. (2012). Sex risk among young men who have sex with men who use Grindr, a smartphone geosocial networking application. *Journal of AIDS and Clinical Research, 3*(SPL Issue 4).

Rosenfeld, M. J., & Thomas, R. J. (2012). Searching for a mate: The rise of the internet as a social intermediary. *American Sociological Review, 77*(4), 523–547.

Roth, Y. (2014). Locating the "Scruff Guy": Theorizing body and space in gay geosocial media. *International Journal of Communications, 8,* 2113–2133.

Ryan, P. (2003). Coming out, fitting in: The personal narratives of some gay men. *Irish Journal of Sociology, 12*(2), 68–85.

Ryan, P. (2016). #Follow: Exploring the role of social media in the online construction of male sex worker lives in Dublin, Ireland. *Gender, Place & Culture, 23*(12), 1713–1724.

Ryan, P., & Ward, E. (2017). Ireland: The rise of neo-abolitionism and the new politics of prostitution. In S. Jahnsen & H. Wagenaar (Eds.), *Assessing prostitution policies in Europe*. Milton Park: Routledge.

Sanders, T. (2008). Male sexual scripts: Intimacy, sexuality and pleasure in the purchase of commercial sex. *Sociology, 42*(3), 400–417.

Sanders, T., Scoular, J., Campbell, R., Pitcher, J., & Cunningham, S. (2018). *Internet sex work: Beyond the gaze*. Cham: Palgrave.

Scoular, J., & O'Neill, M. (2007). Regulating prostitution: Social inclusion, responsibilization and the politics of prostitution reform. *The British Journal of Criminology, 47,* 764–778.

Scott, J. (2003). A prostitute's progress: Male prostitution in scientific discourse. *Social Semiotics, 13*(2), 179–199.

Scull, M. (2013). Reinforcing gender roles at the strip show: A qualitative analysis of men who dance for women (MDW). *Deviant Behaviour, 34,* 557–578.

Stempfhuber, M., & Liegl, M. (2016). Intimacy mobilised: Hook-up practices in the location-based social network Grindr. *Österreichische Zeitschrift für Soziologie, 41,* 51–70.

Styles, J. (1979). Outsider/insider: Researching gay baths. *Urban Life, 8*(2), 135–152.

Thompson-Bonner, C. (2017). The meat market: Production and regulation of masculinities on the Grindr grid in Newcastle-upon-Tyne, UK. *Gender, Place & Culture, 24*(11), 1611–1625.

Tziallas, E. (2015). Gamified eroticism: Gay male 'social networking' applications and self-pornography. *Sexuality and Culture, 19,* 759–775.

Valentine, G. (2006). Globalising intimacy: The role of information and communication technologies in maintaining and creating relationships. *Women's Studies Quarterly, 34*(8), 776–793.

Vanwesenbeeck, I. (2012). Prostitution push and pull: Male and female perspectives. *Journal of Sex Research, 50*(1), 11–16.

Walby, K. (2012). *Touching encounters: Sex, work & male-for male internet escorts.* Chicago: University of Chicago Press.

Woods, W. J., Tracy, D., & Binson, D. (2003). Number and distribution of gay bathhouses in the United States and Canada. *Journal of Homosexuality, 44*(3–4), 55–70.

Woods, W. J., Sheon, N., Morris, J. A., & Binson, D. (2013). Gay bathhouse HIV prevention: The use of staff monitoring of patron sexual behaviour. *Sexuality Research and Social Policy, 10,* 77–86.

4

Instagram, Micro-Celebrity and the World of Intimate Strangers

Abstract Ryan explores how Instagram offers a platform to perform strategies of micro-celebrity to cultivate and grow followers online. These strategies create intimacy, trust and authenticity. Ryan shows how through in-app technology like Instagram Story, polling and direct messaging, followers form para-social interactions with the micro-celebrities they follow. Instagram acts as a gateway to encourage followers to seek greater levels of intimacy through the purchase of monetized content.

Keywords Instagram · Micro-celebrity · Para-social interaction · Intimacy

Introduction

Instagram offered male sex workers a platform with which to construct and showcase their digital lives. If Grindr, as I have argued, offered sex workers a transient and opportunistic means to ambiguously advertise sexual services that were decoded and read by potential clients, Instagram offered entry into a more permanent and intimate digital

© The Author(s) 2019
P. Ryan, *Male Sex Work in the Digital Age*,
https://doi.org/10.1007/978-3-030-11797-9_4

biography. On Instagram, sex workers moved from abstract disembodied muscularity, to men located within a context of their friendships and family relationships but also, crucially, through their consumption of food, travel, clothes and fitness. These profiles communicated the lives of men with a lifestyle, a personhood and an identity. These profiles offered intimate access, a view backstage into the everyday practices that had shaped, not just their bodies, but their lives as newly arrived migrants in Ireland. I argue that my interviewees carefully choreographed these lives, deploying strategies of micro-celebrity interaction to create an illusion of intimacy and of knowing. The in-app features facilitated this. Instagram Story, allowing daily video updates that brought followers through their lives, from morning to night.

This chapter focuses primarily on the lives of three of my interviewees with the largest social media following; Renzo, a 23-year-old full-time student from Venezuela with over 60,000 Instagram followers, Joao, a 27-year-old student from Brazil who worked part-time as a waiter and a personal trainer had over 40,000 and Victor, a 25-year-old also from Brazil had over 35,000 followers. The chapter explores how these men navigate the world of social media to maintain and grow their followers, avoiding the challenges of context collapse (Marwick and Boyd 2011), as they broadcast material to diverse audiences while engaging in micro-celebrity interaction that created gateways to further intimacy. I argue that while followers of Renzo, Joao and Victor have open access to the uploaded material on Instagram, this only serves as the entry point into accessing monetised content by offering a passage through different spheres of intimacy that will provide ever more personalised (and paid) content through sites like Amazon Wish List and OnlyFans. The success of my interviewees in getting payment for content rests in their ability to cultivate followers—or fans—through their own self-branding (Page 2012). With platforms like OnlyFans offering everyone the chance to broadcast content to paid subscribers—it is those with the greatest ability to self-brand that stand to reap the benefits of this 'amateur turn' within the sex industry.

The New Digital Age

The rise of the visual in contemporary society continues unabated. The affordability of smartphones facilitating the taking and dissemination of photographs combined with the popularity of social media platforms, particularly that of photo-sharing sites like Instagram and Snapchat, has consolidated the visual turn in society (Walsh and Baker 2017: 1185). While the motivations in joining sites like Facebook remain complex, its popularity has been premised upon the accumulation of social capital through social networking. User profiles were platforms for self-expression (Van Dijck 2013), fostering different types of sexual or ethnic identity (Bouvier 2012: 42) or more commonly communicating identity through lifestyle and commodification (Doyle 2015). It heralded a more participatory, more democratic style with consumers active in the creation of content, reshaping the balance of power in a digital era (Page 2012: 182). Since the launch of social media sites like Facebook in 2004, the attention economy has grown unabated, rewarding those who strategically use their visibility and influence for economic gain.

There is little dispute that newer social media sites, particularly Instagram have accelerated this process and become more about self-promotion and leveraging social capital present within wide social networks into commercial opportunity. This shift in how individuals seek to use social media sites to construct their identities has contributed, I argue, to a greater choreography in the managed presentation of their digital lives. This has a number of consequences. It has led to the emergence of a spatial self (Schwartz and Halegoua 2014: 2), where lives are not just documented through visual representation, but also now through the user's mobility through space and place recording locations at hotels, restaurants and bars, both locally and throughout the world. It has also led to the rise and fall of the selfie—linguistically at least (Senft and Baym 2015). Selected as the word of the year in only 2013 by the Oxford English Dictionary to convey the spontaneous photographic self-portrait at arm's length, it is now greeted with derision and fatigue (Tiidenberg and Gomez Cruz 2014: 78), particularly by a younger generation but who routinely invest time and energy into staged self-photography, often enhanced by filter technology. It is a practice that has established itself as a genre, complete with visual conventions and techniques shared amongst fellow users (Marwick 2015: 141). It is a practice that has divided academic opinion as either a sign of narcissism[1] or holding the potential to be a vehicle of empowerment, especially for women in regaining control over the production of their images (Gomez Cruz and Miguel 2012). Ordinary users of Instagram would draw upon the use of self-photography within celebrity culture which sought to bypass traditional intermediaries like managers and publicists and speak directly to their fan base in an unmediated communication that offered an uncensored insight into their lives.

Celebrity

The increased interest in the study of celebrity provides some useful concepts to understand the relationship between male sex workers' use of Instagram and the relationship between their followers. My interviewees are heavily socially networked individuals, living out lives for an audience of thousands on a range of social media applications. They are the authors and curators of their own lives, embodying a late modern demand placed upon the individual to continuously reflect and recast the construction of their own identities, drawing upon resources of modern capitalism as they do. Crucially, these men are not just consumers of resources, they are the authors of their own content (Marshall 2014: xxxiii), broadcasting their consumption of commodities, travel and fashion to a diverse and global audience. They have become 'micro-celebrities' or celetoids (Rojek 2001: 20) living their short lives in the spotlight, as influencers, often receiving endorsements to promote particular products in their profiles. They use social media to perform celebrity, enabling the construction of identities, building and maintaining their audience. This has been facilitated by camera and video mobile phone technology that has transformed how these sex workers communicate to their diverse followers, including their potential clients.

The origins of celebrity have been traced to the establishment of the court of Elizabeth 1, and the subsequent transformation of London into a centre of consumerism in the eighteenth century (Inglis 2010: 6; Van Krieken 2012: 16). The World Exhibition in London in 1851 and in Paris four years later, provided a showcase for consumer products that filtered down into newly established department stores (Inglis 2010: 65). The mass production of entertainment, like theatre, created new stars of the stage, made famous through mass-produced newspapers, who would also use them as fodder for gossip columnists. Writers like Chris Rojek (2001: 13) see the emergence of celebrity within this 'democratization of society' where rising literacy amongst the public at large and the growth of a regional press, beyond London contributed to the mass circulation of printed material and saw the 'rise of the public face'. The exponential growth of celebrity could be understood within a more modernist framework, where the mass circulation of television, news and magazines would create an environment where celebrity endorsement would infiltrate every aspect of society, from politics to the economy. Celebrity would also simultaneously mirror the institutional decline of religion and monarchy, filling the vacuum they left in their wake. In this way, celebrity was contributing to a new integrative function within secular societies (Rojek 2001: 13–14). Finally, celebrity culture would also grow in tandem with the rise of consumer capitalism, where new methods of production and distribution, would create new means for showcasing individuality and group alliances becoming markers of class distinction (Van Krieken 2012: 24, 53). Celebrity culture itself would fuel commodification through its embodiment and humanising of desire (Rojek 2001: 187). The advent of new social media applications has elevated this humanisation to a new level.

Intimate Strangers

Late modern societies are characterised by an increasing number of relationships that can be termed as 'weak ties' as opposed to 'strong'. Sociologists like Goffman (1963), Granovetter (1973) and Milgram (1992) all wrote of the need societies have for a combination of strong and weak ties to ensure sufficient, but not excessive integration and cohesion. These 'familiar strangers' (Milgram 1992: 67) that are part of our daily lives remain in a form of stasis, that occasionally spring into life, often at times of emergency and crisis when people experience or witness a traumatic event. Our use of social media has greatly expanded our network of weak ties, when we digitally connect, though not necessarily communicate with, a wide range of individuals than expand outwards from the core relationships of our lives. Bringing 'intimate strangers' into our digital lives, for example, friends of friends, and individuals that are visible within the wider public sphere, from politicians, musicians, actors and authors has become a defining characteristic of how we conduct our new online lives. Horton and Wohl (1956: 215) coined the phrase 'para-social interaction' to understand this relationship between the viewer and a television presenter or performer in the 1950s. Although non-reciprocal and 'not susceptible of mutual development' (p. 215), the performer's presentational style is crucial in creating an interactive experience in which viewers cultivate an emotional relationship they understand to be personal to them. Performers' acts of emotional disclosure strengthened this bond with their viewers who felt they had come to 'know' them as they would in a real interactive relationship (p. 216). Later research that has utilised the concept of para-social interaction has identified that the perceived attractiveness of the presenter or performer is crucial in creating this more personalised experience (e.g. Schramm and Hartmann 2008). This insight is important as I explain the relationship between the young men in my study and their thousands of followers.

Celebrities have been at the vanguard of social media practices that have sought to create new public intimacy while leveraging followers for self-branding and commercial opportunities. This has involved rebranding traditional and highly regulated celebrity management to embrace a more interactive engagement with fans where intimacy, authenticity and access are all performed for a wide audience and market (Marwick and Boyd 2011: 140). Social media like Twitter are used by celebrity to communicate to fans, and other celebrities, to address rumours and allegations and to 'strategically manage self-disclosure', creating an illusion of intimacy and closeness (p. 147). Twitter hashtags are also used to promote corporations, products and slogans and have become a widespread celebrity practice (Page 2012: 198).

Micro-Celebrities

Micro-celebrities embody a range of presentational strategies to construct an online profile, giving access to intimate parts of their digital lives to build up, communicate with and sustain their followers. Senft (2008: 25) defines it as a 'new style of online performance in which people employ webcams, video, audio, blogs and social networking sites' to achieve communication with a networked community. It involves a 'strategic and concerted cultivation of an audience through social media' (Khamis et al. 2016: 6) in the hope of achieving a celebrity status that can lead to sponsorship and monetised content. Their relationship with their followers is different to regular users of social media whom they see primarily as *fans* rather than friends or followers (Marwick 2013: 115). Success within the world of micro-celebrity is dependent on creating intimacy with fans through the disclosure of personal information that creates an impression of closeness in a similar way of achieving para-social interaction identified by Horton and Wohl (1956). It is the 'celebrification of a private self'—suggesting a backstage view into a public life. Marwick (2013: 117–119) identifies some key elements that have defined the practice of micro-celebrity; firstly a self-commodification where the profile is constructed and marketed towards achieving a larger audience, secondly demonstrable intimacy by communicating and interacting with fans and thirdly, this interaction has to take place in a manner in which fans deem to be 'authentic'.

Authenticity is, of course, largely subjective but Marwick's (2013: 119–120) study reveals it is identified by consistency—is current material consistent with material that has been previously posted online? Finally, micro-celebrities have to incorporate a form of 'aspirational consumption' to fans—through mimicking the more glamorous lives of 'real' celebrities. Often there is a crossover between sponsored and non-sponsored content, with Ruan's (2016: 187) study of trans vloggers revealing an uneasy relationship between activism and monetised content, with fears that being perceived as economically motivated would push viewers away. Companies utilise micro-celebrities to build a more direct connection with consumers, hoping that endorsements will translate into increased levels of trust associated with their brands (Djafarova and Trofimenko 2018: 3).

Instagram

Instagram is a free, photo-sharing mobile application launched in 2010 that allows users to upload photos directly from their phones. There are a variety of edit and filter functions—many replicating a nostalgic and retro style format (Marwick 2015: 144)—available to users before they finally decide to upload the photo of their choice. In 2016, Instagram Stories was launched, allowing users to upload a displayed photo or video for one minute which disappears after 24 hours, mirroring the capabilities of Snapchat. Stories allow users to continually add content throughout the day, creating a daily 'story' of the user's life. Instagram profiles can be either private, requiring permission to see the content, or more commonly open to the public, who can follow a user by simply clicking the follow button. This allows users to scroll through recently uploaded photos of their followers of which they can choose to like or comment. Instagram's popularity has been dramatic, achieving 400 million active users in 2016 (Schwartz and Halegoua 2014: 8; Giannoulakis and Tsapatsoulis 2016: 115), and 1 billion monthly users in 2018, far outstripping growth rates of Facebook and Snapchat.[2] The home display screen has space to write a short biography and shows the number of posts a user has uploaded, the numbers of followers and the number following the account.

Users can connect to others through a search function for a specific profile or through the use of hashtags, which were added to Instagram in 2011, that connect users globally who are interested in the same topic. Since 2015, emoji can also be used as hashtags. Hashtags, first introduced by Twitter, and now popular across social media including Instagram, serve two purposes—they label a photograph for search purpose and also provide some explanatory or contextual information to a photo (Scott 2018: 58; Giannoulakis and Tsapatsoulis 2016: 116).

Instagram and Male Sex Work

All of the men I interviewed were active users of Instagram. Their stories revealed different strategies to accumulate followers and publicise their profiles as a platform for soliciting clients. Just as their Grindr profiles were often ambiguous of any sex work intention, relying on other users to read and interpret photos and emoji, their Instagram profiles similarly give no indication of any involvement in sex work. While it would appear judicious to separate the use of Grindr and its association with transient photos and casual sex—paid or otherwise—from Instagram, which provided a more permanent digital record of their lives, a majority of the men (12 out of 18) I interviewed were happy that followers were directed from one profile to the other. Grindr profiles facilitate links to other social media—Twitter, Instagram and Facebook—should users choose to use it. The motivation in allowing viewers migrate between their profiles was complex. Drawing from the men's stories, I outline below three advantages Instagram offered over other social media applications.

1. *Consuming Identity and Personhood*
   Social media profiles offered the men platforms with which to showcase their bodies and their lifestyles, connect to and manage a wide network of followers or fans, some of which could be leveraged for economic gain. Grindr offered limited opportunity to cultivate a following and deploy the micro-celebrity practices I spoke of earlier in this chapter, to achieve a status of sufficient visibility to attract

commercial opportunities. Grindr, offering users just one photo, which is regularly updated, on an app itself that is frequently deleted and reinstalled by users, created a transient community of followers. As I outlined in the previous chapter, this transience allows male sex workers to connect with clients in Dublin and when they travel abroad. It remains largely one-dimensional. Directing potential clients and other users to Instagram opened the door to a multidimensional world of their lives, inviting viewers inside to see their friends, vacations, workouts, nights out, often in real time with Instagram Story. This use of Instagram developed organically. Leo (25) describes how his early Instagram posts were 'me and my friends, at the beach and parties ... I'm not sure when it became more about me, there is more [photos] of me now'. Victor (25) also saw his Instagram as a platform that had evolved over time, also unable to pinpoint when he started to post more strategically to gain additional followers and potential income. Instagram allowed men to create a personhood and identity beyond the caricatures so commonly associated with sex work and mostly frequently denied to female workers in particular. This personhood is achieved through what is conceptualised as *context collapse*, where users speak and deliver content to a diverse range of followers (Marwick and Boyd 2011; Kaul and Chaudhri 2017). Sex work remains the known unknown on Instagram.

2. *Creating Desire Through 'Knowing'*

While the Internet is awash with free and anonymous naked male content, why would social media followers of sex worker profiles pay to see content that is often merely sexually suggestive? I argue that my respondents have cultivated desire amongst their fans through selected self-disclosure that creates a sense of 'knowing' that increases sexual desire. Rather than fixating on an anonymous object of sexual desire, my respondents' profiles draw followers into an ongoing social media relationship which takes them on their journey with these young men on their adventure in Europe. Desire is created through layers of *knowing*—seeing the men in routine photos with friends, photos of them at the gym and through more revealing photos on Instagram Story, where users can target a list of viewers while hiding the stories from others. The strategic and measured access to sexual content also plays a key role in heightening this desire, drawing followers into social media relationships that promise continually greater intimate access to their lives.

3. *Facilitating Sponsorship and Paid Content in the Attention Economy*
Instagram facilitated my respondents' engagement in self-branding through the cultivation of a public image. This was achieved through building a fan base by communicating a distinct public image and a willingness to engage with and meet the needs and expectations of followers that will in turn attract the interest of advertisers (Sanders et al. 2018: 39; Cunningham et al. 2018: 52; Khamis et al. 2016: 190). These opportunities arise within a strong culture of neoliberal individualism, which encourages self-branding as a means to assert independence and control at times of economic precariousness. Companies offering sponsorship in return for product endorsement approached Renzo, Joao and Victor, all of whom were, so far, dissatisfied with the deals, which offered them a substantial discount on the products and a discount code of 15% for their followers. This was deemed not worth the potential negative impact a sponsored profile might have on their ability to retain followers. Later in this chapter, I explore alternative means with which these men generated income, without adopting sponsorship.

Communicating Intimacy

Given the high level of daily usage reported by Instagram users, the site offered the men I interviewed the potential to reach their followers on a regular basis. This communication had traditionally been direct private messaging or posted comments underneath uploaded photos, but Instagram Story has revolutionised interaction, increasing the number of direct messages to users. The use of Instagram Story, introduced at the time I was doing this research, allowed my respondents to update followers on their daily activities, without it becoming part of their permanent digital record. These Story photos were chosen more spontaneously because of this transiency and also were more likely to contain a more suggestive sexual content, although they were moderated by community guidelines that prohibited naked photos. They also encourage a chronology of photos—some of which later appear as a permanent photo on their profiles.

#Iwokeuplikethis

The Instagram Story feature has allowed users to accelerate the micro-celebrity potential of the site, by facilitating a quicker turnover of content, create more interactive opportunities and an enhanced level of intimacy. This capability was further enhanced in 2018, when followers were allowed to ask questions directly of those that they were following, which could then be posted as a Story for others to read. Those men that I interviewed who were the most regular users of this feature favoured bookending their days with photos taken in bed.

> *Renzo (23)*: Sometime it is when I have the most time to post, when I wake up and I'm trying to get out of bed and when I'm listening to music in bed before sleeping, I would post then … I use the #iwokeuplikethis because guys see that photo first when they wake up, doesn't everybody check it [Instagram] in the morning?
>
> *Leo (25)*: The morning and night is good and I post them in bed, when can you post photos without your shirt and they think you are not showing it off – in bed *(laughs)* … guys message more too, I think other people look at this time too, well in Europe.

During the day, the most common photo posted either on Story or on their profiles were from the gym. I outlined in the previous chapter the level of time and energy invested in body projects like the gym, and the photos reflect different aspects of this work. The most common photos were selfies taken in gym mirrors, photos or videos taken by their friends of them working out or post workout photos taken in the gym changing room. The purpose of these photos was less clear. Undoubtedly, these photos contributed to 'creating desire' amongst followers directed to their profiles from Grindr and/or who were interested in meeting sex workers. It was common for those men I interviewed, to suggest that these gym photos were essentially for their private consumption, although public to others, in order to track their fitness progress. Making the photos visible was suggested as an incentive created by the men to help them achieve their goals.

> *Victor (25)*: It is good for me when I am training and before summer and Circuit[3] [festival] to post a photo before I start and then when I finish, everyone sees it and I feel I have to do it and achieve my goals. I tell my fans what I am eating, so people can do it with me, sometimes they send me their photos too, it is good, and we are in it together.

These photos are accompanied by a range of fitness-related hashtags like #gaybrazil #follow #fit #body #6pack #sixpack #flexing #flex #sweatpants #gaylatino #instagay #instamale. The body transformation photo is often accompanied by Stories showing food purchases, cooking and Tupperware boxed food for the day ahead.

#Aboutlastnight

These photos or stories were usually posted and hashtagged the day after a night spent in bars or clubs with friends. Renzo (23) had taken a series of these photos over the last two years in club bathrooms— the format of which remains the same—he is shirtless staring into the mirror at the sink. The composition differs slightly; sometimes he is alone, others there are other nightclub patrons washing their hands on either side or walking inconspicuously behind him. Some are hashtagged #fans and show other club patrons with their arms around him staring at the camera. While the fellow patrons are invariably flushed and sweaty from the club, Renzo always remains composed, groomed and in control—reflecting the 'official accredited values of the society' (Goffman 1959: 23)—youth, beauty and muscularity. Across the interviewees, the photos have a more conventional format, with the men pictured with their friends enjoying their nights out.

#Takemeback

These photos and the accompanying hashtags allowed vacation photos to be sporadically posted throughout the year, particularly in winter and facilitated the use of shirtless beach photos on their profiles outside the summer months. Travel photos focus heavily on transit, rather than traditional sightseeing photos of the destination. The most frequent Story photos included printed boarding cards and passports, with Renzo (23) who frequently flies business class showing a 1A or 2B seat allocation, photos of boarding gate departure screens and luggage. When Renzo and Joao are on tour there are photos of them on trains, most often connecting between Zurich and Vienna. All three men have a near identical photos of themselves working on beach front gym equipment in Barcelona. The focus of these photos is nearly always themselves. Renzo, who uploaded a number of photos from a trip to South Africa with his then boyfriend, included no photos of him from the trip. This permits viewers to have an undistorted gaze of sexual and romantic availability upon Renzo, than photos with his boyfriend would permit. The construction of Renzo, Victor and Joao's profiles are formulaic where there is little deviation between these three photo themes I have outlined above. There are similar silences across the profiles too, there is no reference of politics, for example, at a time when their countries were going through considerable political turmoil.

Managing Micro-Celebrity Interaction

Managing social media profiles like Instagram constitutes a form of affective labour. In addition, eleven of the eighteen men I interviewed also had a Twitter and Snapchat account, spending on average 21 hours a week uploading content, checking other user content and replying to and managing interaction with followers. This investment of time was deemed necessary to maintain existing followers and gather new ones. Choosing content that met the expectations of followers, especially those most likely to pay, was the priority, over other audiences. Inadvertently, some content did alienate existing followers:

Joao (27): Do I get it wrong? Sometimes, I care, I don't care, sorry not sorry … I was at a party at Pride and I posted a Story of me wearing a drag queen's shoe, high heels and it cost me around a 1000 followers – it was a joke, I don't wear things like that but fans really don't like it.

Renzo (23): I posted from Tel Aviv Pride last year and I definitely lost some followers, I had guys message me with links to what was happening in Gaza and building houses on the land of the Palestinians and some messages from Irish guys that I should be ashamed … they think I'm stupid though, a South American Barbie that does not know the world. I know, I chose to go.

Renzo, Joao and Victor, as 'actors within networked publics', have to navigate invisible audiences, blurring boundaries between private and public and *context collapse* (Kaul and Chaudhri 2017: 2; Marwick and Boyd 2011). Rather than pitching their content, as in a face-to-face interaction, when they know the language and cultural context, when online they have to understand this imagined audience (Marwick and Boyd 2011: 115). For example, Renzo, Joao and Victor very rarely attach Spanish or Portuguese messages or hashtags to their posts—their imagined audience in this regard is global and is communicated to through English. Their online content is also viewed by a wider, invisible audience that may often not want to leave a digital trace by following or liking photos of a specific profile, but may connect directly to pay for content. Looking through the follower lists of the three men, reveals an indication of the audience—fitness gym guys in Sydney to teenage girls in Ohio—but not in its entirety, as all three accounts are open to the wider public. Knowing ones audience and speaking strategically to it is a key micro-celebrity interaction.

Scholars have previously tried to understand social media users imagined audience when they tweet or post online to avoid context collapse (Marwick and Boyd 2011). Litt and Hargittai's (2016: 7) analysis of social media users found they had both an abstract imagined audience, but often became focused upon the self-presentation of the act of posting, rather than a real consideration of the audience. There was also a more targeted audience, where users posted to specific audiences. Renzo, Joao and Victor also alternated posts between specific audiences; for example, they all recognised that food posts discussing protein, calorie and fat content were niche to their fitness followers who sought (and paid for) detailed diet plans, compared to generic photos of their bodies at the gym that were viewed through an erotic lens by a wider audience. Maintaining the balance was crucial in retaining followers. My respondents also had to navigate the potential for context collapse, a term drawing from Goffman (1958) to explain how social actors tailor their performances and later used within journalism to illustrate the consequences of addressing multiple audiences with diverse ideas (Kaul and Chaudhri 2017: 4). Currently adopted by scholars of social media (Wesch 2009) to explain how social media flattens multiple audiences into one and 'makes it impossible to differ self-presentation strategies, creating tension' (Marwick and Boyd 2011: 122). Joao and Renzo's stories about Tel Aviv Pride and the use of drag speak to this difficulty in managing audiences. Similar to Marwick and Boyd (2011: 125), my three respondents did self-censor, in subtle ways, with Renzo describing that 'you don't want to be too sexy, guys won't like this stuff cause their followers can check [who they have liked] so you have to be sexy by accident or is it accidentally sexy?' Joao also described the experience of changing his Instagram content and the impact on his followers when he started dating someone:

> It was not a big change, it was slow, I just didn't want to have to keep playing the sexy Latin boy, so I stopped posting some photos, like when I was at the pool, I post the gym photos but it was different … I did lose some [followers] but not many, most people stayed

All three of my respondents felt that there were some expectations governing interaction that they observed. Responding with @replies to a public message of appreciation left under an uploaded photo on Instagram was deemed necessary to signal to other followers a willingness to interact and answer questions, although all felt this was time-consuming. Also time-consuming was removing inappropriate messages left under photos with Joao stating 'you always have to look after you get a notification, just in case they have said something bad or something about sex and then you can delete'. Responding to comments on Instagram Story was deemed different because their messages were private and could be easily ignored:

Victor (25): It is not possible really [to answer Story messages] there are too many and they are just a flower or a heart or something so I ignore them … I only reply to a question like if they ask me my travel schedule, when will you be in Singapore or something like this or a message that want to see more or they ask 'how do I see more of you?', I reply to this too

There is the option to turn off the ability to send messages to Story, but the men felt that this again signalled a lack of willingness to engage and, Renzo describes, 'play by the rules'. These rules seem rather opaque and deciphering them seems to illustrate an intuition amongst my respondents to identify 'time wasters' early, then ceasing to communicate. Like in the previous chapter on Grindr, screening for 'time wasters' is based on recognising a type of questioning that is either too sexual or too demanding of interaction. Renzo felt that men who would ultimately pay for extra content would not demand it—'they are polite, always, and I think talk with respect and talk to get what they want to see, not just chat, chat, chat'. This screening of interaction is similar to those exercised by gay users of social media, including male sex workers (McLean 2013: 80; Race 2015: 260).

Some men following my respondents' Instagram profiles become avid fans. These types of fans were often the most financial lucrative in their willingness to purchase online content and the interaction remained largely unproblematic. Their communication was, however constant, replying to every Story and every uploaded photo often expressing love, admiration and friendship. My respondents struggled to maintain boundaries between public and private digital selves, particularly with men who had purchased their online content. Renzo (23) describes here his 'public' Instagram profile and the extent to which a fan can 'know' him from it:

It's about me but you don't know me from looking – what do you know from photos? A guy with abs that likes Louis Vuitton *(laughs)* it's nothing, not me, my fans don't want that anyway, they want to see my body, my trainers … I don't need them [Instagram] to get business but guys get to see new photos … I'm on their phone when they wake up in the morning, on their bus and some guys will turn from watchers to meeters

And later describing his efforts to conceal this private self:

> They know that my Instagram is only part of me, they know it isn't where I talk to my school friends or my cousins, this guy keeps asking me for my 'real' Instagram but I say I only have one and this is true but I have Facebook for my family and close friends but I changed the name a little so guys wouldn't find it ... it's boring actually ... my grandma's birthday, I don't know why they want to see it so badly

Enguix and Gomez-Narvaez's (2018: 121) respondents, in their study on Instagram, also reported the use of this constructed character rather than the true self. This transformation of private and public boundaries within photography is interesting here, particularly in the light of digital photography. Goffman's (1979: 10) original formulation of photography remains largely intact, albeit slightly inverted, where private photos 'are designed for display within the intimate social circle' celebrating family occasions and events like birthdays and graduations. Walsh and Baker (2017: 1187) rightly point to the contradiction of ceremonial events taking place in public, labelled as private which in turn furnish the domestic sphere. For Goffman (1979: 11), public photos are then destined to become the most widely distributed becoming official representations of individuals, finding their way into magazines and newspapers. Digital photography has transformed this. For Renzo, as illustrated in his previous quote, the photos of his grandmother's 80th birthday party represent for him private photos he is unwilling to share with a wider public. It is the quintessentially private act of being photographed partially naked in a changing room mirror that becomes the 'public' photo because for Renzo, his body is indeed public and represents a physical and erotic capital that he has traded upon since he was a teenager. These changing room photos are constituted as public, also because the intention behind the photo was never a private one—the photos were taken with the intention of the widest possible dissemination. It is false to view these photos exclusively as an expression of Renzo's narcissism—they are interactional—to be traded, admired and ultimately to dominate others who have not yet achieved the prescribed standards of youth, beauty and muscularity. Separating audiences and tailoring content on social media according has been recognised as a strategy particularly amongst LGBTQ communities (Duguay 2016: 900).

Other messages from these fans alternated between personal questions about my respondents' lives, work and relationship status and darker questions about their willingness to engage in financial domination with them. Renzo, Joao and Victor had all received messages asking them to engage in the fetish of financial domination where men would pay tributes or gifts to others while assuming a submissive relationship, a practice made popular under hashtags like #paypig and #cashwhore. I discuss in more detail in the next chapter the financial opportunities derived from having micro-celebrity status on social networking sites like Instagram. Like I discussed in Chapter 3, my respondents were also subject to abuse on Instagram when they refused or ceased to interact with fans or when they were asked to pay for content to advance their interaction with my respondents. Renzo, like the others, remained sanguine about this abuse suggesting that there 'was many crazy people online, you have to deal with it, or get offline and go do yoga', a view shared by Jones' (2016: 245) interviews with webcam models who believed that, 'trolls come with the job'. Even when there has been an unauthorised distribution of photos he circulated to select followers, he remained resigned to the lack of control he could expect to exercise over the distribution of such material he created, although he does go to great lengths to conceal his face in certain photos and videos. Although Renzo, Joao and Victor demonstrate the entrepreneurship that the neoliberal gig economy demands, their belief that they have contributed to their own online harassment is depressing and suggests a victim blaming culture so prevalent in the wider sex industry.

This resignation and lack of sympathy reflected a wider societal response to leaked celebrity nude photos, where responsibility was seen to lie with the producer of the images, rather than those hack and distribute them (Marwick 2017: 185). There is also a gendered dimension to the authorised and unauthorised disclosure of nude photos, with Slater's (2016: 2730–2733) research showing a loss of reputation attached to the practice for women as opposed to men. Deploying micro-celebrity practices to generate intimacy often led to the danger of revealing too much personal information subjecting sex workers to harassment. Victor described how on a trip to Galway in the west of Ireland, he had uploaded photos and Stories to Instagram, including the location of his hotel, when he received a number of messages from a follower asking to meet him which he declined. An hour later when he opened his door he found the man who had messaged him standing there:

> It was crazy, I was so angry and I felt stupid ... this guy had come to the hotel and told a guard that he was staying here, it was 1am in the morning and he needed a key, a card to go and he told the woman at the desk he was my friend and she told him my hotel room, he said 'I'm Victor's friend' and she checked my room and gave him the number at 1am? Can you believe that? And he's knocking at my door! He was drunk and I talked to him for 5 minutes and said I would meet him for breakfast to get him away from me ... I shouted at the woman at the desk after and she said she would call the police if I didn't stay calm.

This example of *doxxing*, where individuals or clients research or hack for identifiable information about a sex worker has been identified as a danger of online work (Jones 2016: 245; Henry and Farvid 2017: 120; Sanders et al. 2018: 109).[4] Evidence of the practice which has been used to harass and stalk sex workers reinforces the challenge of creating intimacy while maintaining distance and anonymity at the same time.

The examples of Renzo, Joao and Victor juggling different online audiences suggest the extent of the impression management they undertook in performing their digital lives. This process described by Goffman (1959) of tailoring interaction with 'front stage' and 'back stage' components complicates social interaction, particularly in a social media age of simultaneous audiences. Goffman (1959) provides a framework to understand how social actors navigate front- and backstage areas of their lives as they perform social interaction with each other. Drawing from a tradition of symbolic interactionism (Blumer 1969), this approach illustrates how the self and society are created in interaction with others. Goffman (1959: 37) reminds us that for most social roles 'a particular front has already been established for it' including 'size and looks; posture; speech patterns; facial expressions; bodily gestures' (p. 55). Renzo, Joao and Victor inhabit many social roles—including fitness expert, struggling student, dominant cash master and as I discuss in the next chapter, amateur adult stars.

Conclusion

This chapter illustrates how the use of Instagram by male sex workers offered an alternative and complementary digital platform with which to build a large social media following. Used in conjunction with the gay dating app, Grindr, my respondents filtered a diverse range of followers to their Instagram profiles, where they were offered access into a choreographed online world. The chapter focused on the experience of three of my respondents who had amassed tens of thousands of followers. Deploying micro-celebrity strategies to foster intimacy amongst their followers, Instagram became a key platform with which to brand the digital self, offering advantages over more transient social media sites like Grindr. In-app features like Instagram Story allowed my respondents to open access to different spheres of intimacy—what was available to all followers of the profiles but also more niche and bespoke content broadcast on a monetised basis.

The construction of a personal brand on Instagram was labour intensive. It necessitated broadcasting content that resonated with the majority of an increasingly diverse group of followers, avoiding material that would alienate those who maybe most likely to purchase content. It necessitated navigating online communication that was often abusive or sought to impersonate or distribute my respondents' images without their consent. Instagram did however serve as a platform that created the intimacy necessary to entice followers to make purchases on both Amazon Wish List and OnlyFans platforms, which I discuss in the next chapter.

Notes

1. https://www.theatlantic.com/entertainment/archive/2013/11/of-course-selfies-are-narcissistic/355432/. Accessed October 5, 2018.
2. https://techcrunch.com/2018/06/20/instagram-1-billion-users/. Accessed June 22, 2018.
3. See Alvarez (2008: 181–200) on Circuit festivals and gay gym culture.
4. Jones (2016: 243) recognises different spellings of *doxxing/doxing*.

References

Alvarez, E. (2008). *Muscle boys: Gay gym culture*. New York: Routledge.

Blumer, H. (1969). *Symbolic interactionism: Perspective and method*. Berkeley: University of California Press.

Bouvier, G. (2012). How Facebook users select identity categories for self-presentation. *Journal of Multicultural Discourses, 7*(1), 37–57.

Cunningham, S., Sanders, T., Scoular, J., Campbell, R., Pitcher, J., Hill, K., et al. (2018). Behind the screen: Commercial sex, digital spaces and working online. *Technology in Society, 53,* 47–54.

Djafarova, E., & Trofimenko, O. (2018). 'Instafamous'—Credibility and self-presentation of micro-celebrities on social media. *Information, Communication & Society.* https://doi.org/10.1080/1369118x.2018.1438491.

Doyle, K. (2015). Facebook, Whatsapp and the commodification of affective labour. *Communication, Politics and Culture, 48*(1), 51–65.

Duguay, S. (2016). "He has a way gayer Facebook that I do": Investigating sexual identity collapse on a social networking site. *New Media & Society, 18*(6), 891–907.

Enguix, B., & Gómez-Narváez, E. (2018). Masculine bodies, selfies, and the (Re)configurations of intimacy. *Men and Masculinities, 21*(1), 112–130.

Giannoulakis, S., & Tsapatsoulis, N. (2016). Evaluating the descriptive power of Instagram hashtags. *Journal of Innovation in Digital Ecosystems, 3,* 114–129.

Goffman, E. (1958). *The presentation of the self in everyday life*. New York: Doubleday.

Goffman, E. (1959). *The presentation of the self in everyday life*. London: Penguin Press.

Goffman, E. (1963). *Behaviour in public places*. New York: Free Press.

Goffman, E. (1979). *Gender advertisements*. New York: Harper & Row.

Gomez Cruz, E., & Miguel, C. (2012). Creation and control in the photographic process: iPhones and the emerging fifth moment of photography. *Photographies, 5*(2), 203–221.

Granovetter, M. (1973). The strength of weak ties. *American Journal of Sociology, 78*(6), 1360–1380.

Henry, M. V., & Farvid, P. (2017). 'Always hot, always live': Computer-mediated sex work in the era of 'camming'. *Women's Studies Journal, 31*(2), 113–128.

Horton, D., & Wohl, R. (1956). Mass communication and para-social interaction: Observations on intimacy at a distance. *Psychiatry, 19,* 215–229.

Inglis, F. (2010). *A short history of celebrity*. Princeton: Princeton University Press.

Jones, A. (2016). "I get paid to have orgasms": Adult webcam models negotiation of pleasure and danger. *Signs: Journal of Women in Culture and Society, 42*(11), 227–256.

Kaul, A., & Chaudhri, V. (2017). Do celebrities have it all? Context collapse and the networked publics. *Journal of Human Values, 24*(1), 1–10.

Khamis, S., Ang, L., & Welling, R. (2016). Self-branding, 'micro-celebrity' and the rise of social media influencers. *Celebrity Studies, 8*(2), 191–208.

Litt, E., & Hargittai, E. (2016). The imagined audience on social network sites. *Social Media and Society,* 1–12.

Marshall, P. D. (2014). *Celebrity and power: Fame in contemporary culture*. Minneapolis: University of Minnesota Press.

Marwick, A. E. (2013). *Status update: Celebrity, publicity and branding in the social media age*. New Haven: Yale University Press.

Marwick, A. E. (2015). Instafame: Luxury selfies in the attention economy. *Public Culture, 27*(1), 137–160.

Marwick, A. E. (2017). Scandal or sex crime? Gendered privacy and the celebrity nude photo leaks. *Ethics and Information Technology, 19,* 177–191.

Marwick, A., & Boyd, D. (2011). To see and be seen: Celebrity practice on Twitter. *Convergence: The International Journal of Research into New Media Technologies, 17*(2), 139–158.

Marwick, A. E., & Boyd, D. (2011). I tweet honestly, I tweet passionately: Twitter users, context collapse, and the imagined audience. *New Media & Society, 13*(1), 114–133.

McLean, A. (2013). 'You can do it from your sofa': The increasing popularity of the internet as a working site among male sex workers in Melbourne. *Journal of Sociology, 51*(4), 1–16.

Milgram, S. (1992). *The individual in a social world*. New York: McGraw-Hill.

Page, R. (2012). The linguistics of self-branding and micro-celebrity in Twitter: The role of hashtags. *Discourse & Communication, 6*(2), 181–201.

Race, K. (2015). 'Party and play': Online hook-up devices and the emergence of PNP practices among gay men. *Sexualities, 8*(3), 253–275.

Rojek, C. (2001). *Celebrity*. London: Reaktion Books.

Ruan, T. (2016). *Out online: Trans self-representation and community building on YouTube*. London: Routledge.

Sanders, T., Scoular, J., Campbell, R., Pitcher, J., & Cunningham, S. (2018). *Internet sex work: Beyond the gaze*. Cham: Palgrave.

Schramm, H., & Hartmann, T. (2008). The PSI-process scales: A new measure to assess the intensity and breadth of para-social processes. *Communications—The European Journal of Communication Research, 33*, 385–401.

Schwartz, R., & Halegoua, G. (2014). The spatial self: Location-based identity performance on social media. *New Social Media, 17*(10), 1–18.

Scott, K. (2018). 'Hashtags work everywhere': The pragmatic functions of spoken hashtags. *Discourse, Context & Media, 22*, 57–64.

Senft, T. M. (2008). *Camgirls: Celebrity and community in the age of social networks*. New York: Peter Laing.

Senft, T. M., & Baym, N. K. (2015). What does the selfie say? Investigating a global phenomenon. *International Journal of Communication, 9*, 1588–1606.

Slater, M. (2016). Privates in the online public: Sex(ting) and reputation on social media. *New Media & Society, 18*(11), 2723–2739.

Tiidenberg, K., & Gómez Cruz, E. (2014). Selfies, image and the re-making of the body. *Body & Society, 21*(4), 77–102.

Van Dijck, J. (2013). 'You have one identity': Performing the self on Facebook and LinkedIn. *Media, Culture & Society, 35*(2), 199–215.

Van Krieken, R. (2012). *Celebrity society*. London: Routledge.

Walsh, M. J., & Baker, S. A. (2017). The selfie and the transformation of the public-private distinction. *Information, Communication & Society, 20*(8), 1185–1203.

Wesch, M. (2009). YouTube and you: Experiences of self-awareness in the context of the collapse of the recording webcam. *Explorations in Media Ecology, 8*, 19–34.

5

Netporn and the Amateur Turn on OnlyFans

Abstract Ryan explores how male sex workers use netporn to convert their social media profiles into economic capital. There is a focus on the use of Amazon's gift registry site, Wish List and how it has enabled sex workers to receive gifts for online content on Instagram. Ryan explores how OnlyFans, a subscription based digital platform allows followers to view uploaded content from broadcasters. This has streamlined the manner in which sex workers communicate with their followers, allowing access to further monetised content that promises greater levels of intimacy. Ryan concludes by discussing how this site, which currently benefits those with large social media profiles, affects their relationships with face-to-face clients.

Keywords Netporn · Male sex work · Intimacy · Amazon Wish List

Introduction

In this chapter, I explore two online platforms—Amazon Wish List and OnlyFans—through which the male sex workers converted the strategic cultivation of their digital lives into economic capital.

© The Author(s) 2019
P. Ryan, *Male Sex Work in the Digital Age*,
https://doi.org/10.1007/978-3-030-11797-9_5

These digital lives have been showcased on different social media platforms—each offering varying degrees of intimacy—from the transient pop-up escort of Grindr to the choreographed lifestyle identity of Instagram, inviting followers and fans into their world of fitness, travel, shopping and nightlife. I argue that these spheres of intimacy are managed by a series of gatekeeper interactions with fans, in which Amazon Wish List—a list of consumer items that can be purchased anonymously by a benefactor—has played a central role in monetising access to content. OnlyFans, launched in 2016, allows people to join as either creators or subscribers of content revolutionising digital sex work by creating easy access and payment for those who want to broadcast sexual content.[1] OnlyFans terms and conditions do state however that users may not upload content that 'promotes or advertises escort services'.[2] They represent what Sanders et al. (2018: 47) describe as 'content delivery platforms'. While those that pay for premium content remain small (Edelman 2009), I argue that the rise in micro-celebrity interaction and the desire for intimate engagement have led to an increasing number of followers and fans willing to pay for more bespoke sexual broadcasts, often considerably less explicit than which is available for free online. This arrival of *netporn*—pornographies on online platforms and networks (Paasonen 2010: 1298)—has contributed to a democratisation of the adult film industry where the removal of agents, producers and other intermediaries has allowed those with micro-celebrity followers to monetise sexual content. The traditional porn industry has had to adapt to online piracy and the dramatic rise in amateur stars which have created a smaller 'professional' market, but with more people willing to take those jobs (Berg 2016: 164). Creators of pornography now set the terms under which they work and become the principle beneficiaries of their work. This development has been built upon the interactional trade in sexualised photos and videos online on apps like Grindr and Snapchat, by financially rewarding those with the greatest physical and erotic capital (Hakim 2018). It is a trade that capitalises on the desire for authenticity and intimacy from the viewers of adult content that has led to a large number of newcomers entering this segment of the market redefining the traditional terms associated with the sex industry (Van Doorn and Velthuis 2018). These newcomers are drawn to digital sex work for the recognised benefits including flexible work schedules, promoting physical safety and limiting contact with police (Jones 2015: 785). In my study, it is those with the greatest number of Instagram followers, Renzo, Joao and Victor that have been early adaptors to the technology that has turned them into adult stars.

Pornographisation of Everyday Life

The rise of digital platforms to share and sell sexual content is part of a wider process where the sex industry has become mainstreamed within the economy and society throughout Europe. This process has been understood as reflecting both the size of the sex industry but also the movement into other areas of the economy, for example, hotels benefiting from adult pay-per-view services (Brents and Sanders 2010: 42). Neoliberal economic policies have deregulated local economies and privileged entrepreneurship where values of individual responsibility and the free market are sacrosanct (p. 46). The increased social acceptance of the sex industry is a by-product of this entrepreneurship, where the use of sex to market and sell consumer goods has become ubiquitous across the economy. The changing class profile of both consumers and workers within the sex industry is also contributing to this acceptance, with stories of university students (Sanders and Hardy 2015) and graduates in the industry challenging a more dominant coercive narrative of homelessness or drugs.

Significant changes have also taken place in the understanding of masculinity, where male bodies have become erotised across cultural life, including advertising, fashion and film (MacPhail et al. 2015: 486). As I discussed in Chapter 3, the taking and exchange of naked photos by gay men on dating sites like Grindr have become an indispensable part of how the app is used. It has allowed the body to be showcased and admired, where physical and erotic capital is accumulated to be traded with others. The movement towards the payment of those men with the greatest capital to see their photo and video content is an inevitable consequence.

Netporn and the Search for Authenticity

Passonen (2010: 1299) identifies the defining features of netporn as challenging conventions of traditional pornography targeted towards a male heterosexual audience with both a new political and ethical sensibility. This has privileged a nuanced queer understanding of sexual acts and desires within a framework that aims to challenge exploitative practices in the industry. However, both sides of the sex industry are interrelated. Berg and Penley (2016: 161–162) argue that satellite industries like netporn have long supplemented the earnings of porn stars offering great autonomy, flexibility and control over work schedules. With the porn industry increasingly casting amateurs to meet growing demands for authenticity, wages become depressed, forcing more professionals into the netporn market, competing with new entrants (p. 163). Whether an established or amateur performer, building a personal brand and following on social media are seen as a necessity to survive in the industry (p. 167).

Netporn is also building upon technological developments that are facilitating a more interactive user experience, establishing itself as an alternative medium that is redefining the meaning of pornography. This alternative medium offers a bespoke porn experience—interactive and crafted to individual needs as opposed to traditional mass-produced and passively consumed pornography (Passonen 2010: 1330; Berg and Penley 2016: 168). Sites like the adult webcam platform, Chaturbate, founded in 2011, have been a leader in this field, offering an interface that supports both the broadcast of webcams and allows users to modify and extend applications that can be used on it (Van Doorn and Velthuis 2018: 180). Customers buy tokens used to tips models who later redeem them for cash, while Chaturbate withholds 50% of the income generated to cover administration costs (p. 180). A similar platform, FlirtCam, demands the same 50% of tips received, suggesting it is an industry standard (Weiss 2018: 736; Mathews 2017: 165; Sanders et al. 2018: 29). Competition between models is a key element of Chaturbate and other sites like AsianPlaymates (Mathews 2017: 167), with models ranked on its placement board.

This competition encourages, Van Doorn and Velthuis (2018: 182) argue, a 'race to the bottom' with models vying to become the most extreme to attract a larger number of viewers and tokens or the use of viewbots to artificially increase their viewers, raising their visibility on the platform. Offering a more personable and entertaining performance, although identified as being labour intensive, set models apart from those that did not have the communicative or English language skills to compete for viewers on this basis. It also facilitated the entry of people into sex work who had been rejected by the sex industry, on the grounds of size, looks or age, and were now offering a niche physical appeal (Berg 2016: 161; Berg and Penley 2016: 168). This competition invariably impacted upon the customers who felt they could tip very little but still place specific demands on the models, causing a number of them to close their accounts (Van Doorn and Velthuis 2018: 188). Similarly, models also gave out details of their Amazon Wish Lists to supplement their income, but they have increasingly become a substitute for tokens leading to an overall devaluation of digital sex work (Berg and Penley 2016: 165; Van Doorn and Velthuis 2018: 183).

Webcam models who broadcast longer shows and derived most of their income exclusively from camming were more likely to divulge personal information about themselves, creating an illusion of intimacy with their viewers (Weiss 2018: 738; Mathews 2017: 167). This has become a dominant feature of netporn as it seeks to create a niche identity in opposition to large adult studios. In Weiss' (2018: 739) cyberethnography of male and female models on FlirtCam, there was a willingness to partake in a digital 'girlfriend experience' with customers to achieve this intimacy. Models also regularly deferred their own desires to engage in cam sex that was exciting to their customers, shaving body hair for example, in line with their clients' desires.

Amazon Wish List

Wish List is a public gift registry available to users on the Amazon website. Amazon, founded in 1994, is now the world's largest digital retailer, with its founder Jeff Bezos currently holding the accolade of the world's richest man with a fortune of $151 billion.[3] Users of Amazon can construct their own Wish List profile, listing a range of consumer products that they would like to own, in a manner similar to a wedding gift registry. The name and postal details remain anonymous to viewers and benefactors when they purchase an item from the list. The use of Wish List is identified within the sex industry, with Van Doorn and Velthuis' (2018: 183) webcam respondents sending their lists to customers to supplement income. Sex workers have long complained that Amazon has targeted their accounts deleting them for 'bartering' which is against its terms and conditions.[4] Berg's (2016: 169) research shows how porn performers use Wish List to ask fans to buy clothes like lingerie used in their scenes to offset wardrobe costs not supported by studios. These clothes were often resold online by performers afterwards.

A majority of my respondents (13 out of 18 men) had set up a Wish List account, although the extent to which it was frequently updated and circulated to potential clients varied between them. Respondents like Renzo, Joao and Victor, who had the largest number of social media followers made the greatest use of their Wish List accounts, using them to permit clients to access bespoke material that remained unseen by other fans. Wish List accounts acted as a gatekeeper, permitting clients passage through various spheres of intimacy with the men I interviewed, culminating with nudity. There was some discrepancy in how each man constructed their Wish List in choosing what to include—again, those with the greatest fan following included some high value products tapering down to products worth €20. Renzo and Joao describe how they construct the Wish List.

Joao (25): I think there has to be something that you want but that they [clients] want to see or think about you so I have some Andrew Christian swimwear on mine, so buy it and they can see me in it, everyone is happy … I have trainers on mine, I put a pair of Yeezys on them as well, they are more than €200, I think you have to be not crazy or ask for something crazy but you can't be too cheap, no one likes crazy but no one follows you because you are cheap.

Renzo (23): I put a lot of different things there, I think the most expensive is a mac book, because I want to upgrade so maybe that will happen … mainly its gym stuff – shorts, tops, underwear, I put a wallet on too – it was a lot but you never know

Other men chose to construct a Wish List that was more niche. Daniel (24) who was studying to become a personal trainer placed exclusively fitness related products on his Wish List. He felt that he didn't 'want to look like a greedy queen obsessed with labels' and thought that his Wish List was more authentic, as it offset some of the high cost of protein supplements:

> This is so expensive, if you drink it a few times a day when you are training and when you are not, there is one before gym, with caffeine. It's like Red Bull before you train and after another and then Creatine and other supplements like Omega so it is expensive but I feel if guys want me to look good and look at me well they should pay some of it no? My problem is that it is boring, you know it looks boring, guys want the sexy stuff and what they can see, I also put some Under Armour shorts, they are my favourite but guys always buy these first – how many shorts do I need? *(laughs)* Buy the protein please!

Daniel's experience of Wish List represents some of the identified problems with operating in this pay to view sexual market. While broadcasters do get to choose how they are portrayed, they are also subject to what viewers and subscribers want to see and what they are prepared to pay for (Henry and Farvid 2017: 121). When exactly during an online interaction, the men gave prospective clients their Wish List varied—although nobody advertised it openly on any of their social media accounts. Wish List was deployed by male sex workers at a stage of interaction when fans were demanding to see extra content than what was available to all on their profiles.

Levels of Interaction on Instagram

Most interaction between the men I interviewed and their fans consisted of liking of photos and videos and leaving comments. This most basic of interactions was also the most crucial in gauging the continued engagement of their fans with the content they were broadcasting. As holders of an Instagram business profile, Renzo, Joao and Victor could check the provenance of those *likes*, whether they were drawn from existing fans or from an invisible audience (Kaul and Chaudhri 2017: 2; Marwick and Boyd 2010; Litt and Hargittai 2016) and the country of origin. This information did impact on which hashtags they chose to use or drop and which content connected with a larger audience but crucially, the act of liking photos was a source of vindication for the men and an affirmation of their self-discipline in diet and training. Renzo describes that a photo 'might get a few hundred likes – I love likes, when I put up a new photo I get crazy checking watching it go up'. Renzo's almost obsessive pursuit of more photo 'likes' illustrates what Race (2015: 498) describes as a gay identity that 'takes the form of a compelling mode of everyday distraction, personal validation and social recognition'. Similarly, Hakim (2018: 236) understands photo 'likes' as a measure of accumulated social capital. The professional fitness respondents in his study saw social media validation as essential for economic capital and the progression of their careers. Non-professionals did not see their engagement with social media contributing anything tangible with one interview suggesting that it 'doesn't equate to anything really for the future, for building yourself as a person' (p. 237). The quest for this social recognition intersects with the sexual entrepreneurship (Lane 2000) skills displayed by sex workers like Renzo, who heavily invest in photos and services that adapt and target clients online and offline. For Victor, the feedback 'made it worth the effort' and was 'inspiration to keep going'. However, for Joao these messages, whether in private or public, soon got repetitive—'nice body, nice body, nice body – I just respond to one of this type of message' he told me.

Often messages were more specific, with fans asking more detailed questions about workout programmes and diets. Renzo describes these enquires as 'how can I look like you?' messages:

> Guys message looking for information about what I am eating or what programme I am doing, it is cool, sometimes they try to create this connection and then they are 'show me your cock' so I usually stop chatting or block, but most want to know about the gym and want more photos … I tell them that I send the diet plan and workout but only for a Wish List purchase and guys are OK, well OK some tell me to fuck off *(laughs)* but most buy something cheap – it's cool.

When receiving a request for more photos or specifically nude photos, Renzo, Joao and Victor again deploy the Wish List as a means of getting compensated, using Instagram Story to send a photo or a video that can only be viewed within a limited timescale. All three men agreed that being more sexually suggestive than explicit was the key to maintaining interest and followers. Victor told me that:

> You don't want to show too much, enough but not everything, if they see everything right away they lose interest quickly and they can see everything online you know? They can watch anything they want, they are watching you not for that, it is hard to explain, and they want to pay you not to show them all of you – does that make sense?

Responding individually to such messages and sending photos or videos was time-consuming, especially given that the financial rewards were slim. Renzo, Joao and Victor all did tell of examples where they exchanged photos with fans who did later become real-time clients. Using online platforms to screen clients for real-time meetings has been well established by sex work scholars (e.g. Jonsson and Svedin 2014). The goods secured through Wish List, in line with other research on precarious netporn labour (Berg and Penley 2016: 165; Van Doorn and Velhuis 2018: 183) only constituted a supplementary income for the men I interviewed, necessitating them to continue to work in cafes and restaurants. The launch of OnlyFans in 2016 would change all that.

Onlyfans—'Where Selfies Pay'

This platform targets the creators of content (bloggers, influencers, fitness models, personal trainers and bodybuilders) to register and broadcast to users who pay a monthly subscription fee to view the uploaded material. The platform takes advantage of a number of developments which I have discussed in this chapter. It is marketed as offering bespoke content that suggests greater *authenticity* to users—no production studios, no poorly designed sets or rented apartments, rather subscribers are brought directly into the homes of content producers, more specifically, their bedrooms and bathrooms. It represents a redistribution of power within the sex industry, with broadcasters setting the price of their monthly subscriptions and OnlyFans taking 20% of the income created to cover administrative costs, compared to webcam hosting platforms regularly seeking 50% of all income. The broadcasters that benefit the most from OnlyFans are those that already have a large personal following on social media, or can acquire one—success is premised on the ability to *self-brand* and promote the digital self (Khamis et al. 2016; Marwick 2013; Page 2012). To facilitate this, the platform is currently linked to Twitter and soon to other social media sites and will retweet updates like new followers and new posts on the broadcaster's profile. It encourages broadcasters to 'place your OnlyFans profile link in 'About Me' fields on your social media profiles' to promote their profile and grow their followers. OnlyFans also builds upon the proliferation of the visual society (Walsh and Baker 2017: 1185), encouraging broadcasters in online advertising that promotes the site as—'Where Selfies Pay'.

OnlyFans' twitter account also reminds broadcasters, that unlike other social media platforms, 'we would like to confirm that sexually explicit content is allowed on #OnlyFans and will not be prohibited'.[5] While sex workers heavily use the platform (Twitter replies to the message above were exclusively by sex workers), the advertising of escort services remains prohibited by their terms and conditions. To open an account, broadcasters have to upload a scanned copy of their passport or driver's licence and add their bank account details if resident in the USA, Canada, Australia and the European Union while the availability of e-Payments facilitates citizens from other countries to receive payment. Broadcasters set the subscription fee themselves, the minimum allowed being $4.99 per month, while there is no upper limit $12.99 is the average monthly subscription charged.

OnlyFans was launched at the time I was conducting this research. Those with established social media profiles, especially Renzo, Joao and Victor who form the basis of this chapter, were early adaptors to this technology. It was a topic I returned to interview them about again as the number of their subscribers grew over 2016–2018. I was curious to discover whether an increasing number of subscribers and income derived from them would affect the frequency with which they met face-to-face clients. The success of OnlyFans did cause them to re-evaluate their use of Twitter, for which they had only used for personal use.

> *Victor*: I had only 2,000 followers on Twitter at that time, I didn't spend time there, it was where I watched other guys, porn stars and other guys, it was where I watched and was a fan but I never had my face but I am getting more followers now and I am posting there, I put the [OnlyFans] link there and it is growing there and on Twitter but I tell you that four accounts on social media is too much for me, I can't do it and give all his time.
> *Joao*: I put it [the OnlyFans link] on my Instagram and it worked, I was surprised because you don't tell people what you will put there so guys messaged and say 'what's there?' and I'd just say 'more' … when I use it now sometimes I put the [OnlyFans] name on a [Instagram] Story so it's like – 'you like this? Well pay the 12 euro and see more'

A number of other interviewees were dissuaded from using OnlyFans because they did not have a Twitter account and felt that they did not possess the critical mass of followers necessary to make the management of a profile worthwhile. As a result, other interviewees placed the OnlyFans link in the bio section of their Instagram profiles, although this did risk context collapse as diverse audiences are given access to a link for niche content (Kaul and Chaudhri 2017: Wesch 2009). The use of Twitter is not widespread within the sex industry. The Cunningham et al. (2018: 52) study of sex work and digital space founded that only just under 30% of respondents had a Twitter account, which was skewed towards younger workers and those that were involved in the provision of indirect services like web camming.

Content

The photographic and video footage that Renzo, Joao and Victor uploaded on their OnlyFans accounts was similar to the material that they had used on Instagram Story. This material was now stored permanently on their OnlyFans account and was available to all new subscribers, offering greater time efficiency in how they responded to individual messages. All those who messaged were now referred to the OnlyFans link, largely bypassing Amazon Wish List where access to additional content had previously been negotiated. Advertising OnlyFans accounts did publically locate my interviewees on the spectrum of digital sex work for the first time—although the marketing of OnlyFans does allow ambiguity as to the content. The platform did allow adult film stars to use their notoriety to gain income through subscriptions and escorting that far exceeded the rates they were paid in the traditional porn industry (Berg 2016: 167). Adult film stars used their personal brand as a marketing tool to leverage more income from satellite sex industries. My interviewees were in a different situation. They occupied a nebulous position in sex work's gig economy balancing discretion with a public social media profile to capture enough subscribers to compete with other broadcasters. They are typical of a new middle-class cohort of male and female performers drawn to netporn by the ability to earn money, minimise risk while maintaining flexible work schedules (Jones 2015: 785: Jones 2016: 231). There is not always a connection however between netporn work and face-to-face sex work (see Mathews 2017: 174).

This income, as I discussed in the previous chapter, often went to realising future goals in work, education or training or with a view to return to graduate careers in Brazil or Venezuela sometime in the future. The quotes from Renzo, Joao and Victor below illustrate how they were all navigating their way around the platform in different ways, broadcasting material they thought was consistent with the digital selves they had spent years carefully creating and keeping sexually explicit content private for a select few through the *paid message* function.

> *Renzo*: It is hard for me to be private, which I need for my job and being very well known on social media and having many fans ... I decided what works for me, everyone is different. It is [OnlyFans] a good opportunity for me, I would be stupid not to do it, especially when I see the guys that do ... my videos are all different, some, OK a lot (*laughs*) of me in the gym, working out and then changing in the gym and in the shower, but they are nudes, there is nothing sexual, I'm not shoving

my ass in someone's face or jerking off, it's just nude. I think they are of great taste; I printed one and have it framed in my bedroom … of course I do send some less tasteful ones too *(laughs)* but you have to pay more

Joao: I think a lot of mine are the gym. It is hard because if you do similar things people don't re-subscribe so you are trying to be new and showing something different. Have you seen the piano videos? People love them and I need to get a piano for me because my mother she says 'ah I'm going to rid of that thing, nobody uses it'

Interviewer: Tell me about the piano videos – how did they happen?

Joao: You have seen them man, I play the piano naked … I did it in my house when I visit [Brazil] last year, I play four pieces that I know but now I need some more … I put one up a new one after some months so I need to practice more *(laughs)* But I tell you the truth, they are so popular, guys love them, it's crazy, I think it's my thing … It is what I get most [private] messages about but I can't do anything personal because I don't have the piano? Do you have one? *(laughs)*

Victor: For me, I try to link it to [Instagram] Story to bring people to it [OnlyFans] because I don't have enough followers on Twitter but it works … I can choose who to send it to on Story so not everyone gets it … I'm using the polls now [introduced in 2017] to ask my fans to choose, like what underwear should I wear, what shorts in the gym should I wear, what swimwear and then they can see it on [Only] Fans, people like it … I show more too but I don't show my face when I do that. I use [paid] private messages to send more sexy stuff … jerking off mostly but maybe more if I get a good offer

In telling his story of using the polling feature on Instagram Story, Victor offers another means to which to connect with followers in a manner identified by scholars of micro-celebrity where there is strategic cultivation of the audience in a way deemed to be authentic (Khamis et al. 2016: 6; Marwick 2013: 117–119). Polling offers a direct way for fans to influence future posts of the account they are following. Similarly, Joao's strategy is also central to this cultivation of followers. His piano playing does represent a niche self-branding (Berg and Penley 2016: 168) in a crowded marketplace that has the potential to attract a loyal core following, while speculating that—'I think it's my thing'.

These videos are also clearly a source of pleasure for Joao, with his followers sending him photos of video clips of themselves playing musical instruments naked, creating a situation where 'the performers and the audience are the same people' (Shah 2007: 35).

Income

The earning potential from broadcasting content on Onlyfans does seem to be considerable. Those that have a large social media following are best placed to unlock this potential but even for Renzo, my interviewee with the largest following, persuading those to migrate from Instagram or Twitter was challenging. Renzo has been trying to direct some of his 60,000 Instagram followers to subscribe since opening his Onlyfans account in 2016. I have remained in contact with him over the last two years where his monthly subscription income, including tips from private messages, has ranged from $350 in 2016 to $6735 in 2018. There is no guarantee that this 2018 income figure can be maintained. Renzo describes his subscribers as made up of 'hard-core fans' that remain followers over consecutive years, and those that can be described as 'floaters'—people that move from different broadcasters every month. The challenge for all broadcasters, including Renzo, is to persuade some floaters to stay subscribed while attracting new followers to replace the lost income from cancellations. When I asked him how this extra income has affected his face-to-face client work, he remained cautious—'I don't want to lose clients that I have known for a long time, regular work with good people is so important, but I have definitely stopped seeing more new people'. Both Joao and Victor also earned an increasing monthly subscription income throughout 2016 and 2017 earning a maximum of $2500 and $1600, respectively.[6] All three men told me that they were also cautious about placing sexual online content that had a more permanent digital life than photo-sharing capabilities in Instagram, for example. Operating online does not remove all risk, and I discussed some of those challenges of impersonation and unauthorised distribution, a common experience for all sex workers (Sanders et al. 2018: 109), in previous chapters. These same concerns exist with the use of OnlyFans.

It remains too early to predict the long-term impact of OnlyFans on digital sex work. The platform is successfully filling a vacuum in hosting the explosion of micro-celebrities that has amassed huge followers on Instagram and Twitter by offering them and their subscribers' easy payment solutions to view content. Crucially, it is allowing for the broadcast of sexually explicit material at a time when the community guidelines of sites like Instagram have become more restrictive. OnlyFans continues to develop technologically, now offering broadcasters live streaming options at a more competitive rate, challenging more traditional webcam sites by introducing a real-time dimension to the platform. The marketing of OnlyFans to a broad church of Instagram influencers, bloggers, athletes and models provides a new digital space for sex workers whose successful self-branding facilitates the conversion of not just their bodies but also their everyday sexual lives into monetised content. My interviews reveal that social media users investing time and energy in devising new and innovative content to maintain and grow subscribers can generate an alternative income stream that allows them restrict the number of appointments with face-to-face clients. This does remain the privilege of those most successful at harnessing the platform.

Conclusion

In this chapter, I have argued that changes within the sex industry have facilitated the rise of amateur content broadcast on platforms like OnlyFans. My interviewees revealed how they have been beneficiaries of this amateur turn by leveraging large numbers of social media fans on Instagram and Twitter into paid subscribers on OnlyFans. This development, although experienced only by the most prolific social media users, was influencing the number of face-to-face clients they were seeing expanding the scope of satellite sex industries. The growing popularity of OnlyFans illustrates the trend towards mainstreaming male sex workers on broadcast platforms that include a diverse range of gay and straight users including personal trainers, models and influencers. I locate income derived from the use of sites like OnlyFans and Amazon Wish List within the gig economy as male sex workers combine income as waiters, face-to-face meetings and new opportunities within the growth of netporn.

This chapter revealed the potential dividend of self-branding within social media and the cultivation of followers through micro-celebrity interaction to foster intimacy. While followers and fans demanded greater access and intimacy, my respondents carefully navigated these requests promoting a public profile with photos and videos that offered choreographed insights into vacations, family and friends while maintaining a backstage private life on an alternative social media profile for family and close friends. These attempts were often not enough. While digital sex work is routinely seen as safer, my respondents did tell of stories where divulging too much information about their lives and where they lived, did open them to harassment by followers.

Notes

1. Objections to the rise of digital pornography have largely mirrored those of early anti-pornography feminists like Dworkin (1989) and MacKinnon (1987) who see pornography as a violence against women as opposed to recognising it as a new public sexual culture (Paasonen 2010: 1298) or part of the gig or gift economy.
2. https://onlyfans.com/terms/. Accessed November 18, 2018.
3. https://www.forbes.com/sites/kathleenchaykowski/2018/07/17/jeff-bezos-net-worth-hits-record-151-billion-after-strong-amazon-prime-day/#e-aed1182e802. Accessed July 3, 2018.
4. https://www.dailydot.com/irl/amazon-sex-woker-wish-lists.   Accessed November 23, 2018.
5. https://twitter.com/onlyfansapp?lang=en. Accessed July 5, 2018.
6. I had completed some interviews in 2015 prior to the launch of OnlyFans in 2016. I did manage to follow-up with a number of these interviewees about the site, so I have only a partial insight into their subsequent use of the platform.

References

Berg, H. (2016). 'A scene is just a marketing tool': Alternative income streams in porn's gig economy. *Porn Studies, 3*(2), 160–174.

Berg, H., & Penley, C. (2016). Creative precarity in the adult film industry. In M. Curtin & K. Sanson (Eds.), *Precarious creativity: Global media, local labor* (pp. 159–171). Oakland: University of California Press.

Brents, B. G., & Sanders, T. (2010). Mainstreaming the sex industry: Economic inclusion and social ambivalence. *Journal of Law and Society, 37*(1), 40–60.

Cunningham, S., Sanders, T., Scoular, J., Campbell, R., Pitcher, J., Hill, K., et al. (2018). Behind the screen: Commercial sex, digital spaces and working online. *Technology in Society, 53,* 47–54.

Dworkin, A. (1989). *Pornography: Men possessing women.* New York: Penguin.

Edelman, B. (2009). Red light States: Who buys adult entertainment. *Journal of Electronic Perspectives, 23*(1), 209–220.

Hakim, J. (2018). 'The spornosexual': The affective contradictions of male body-work in neo-liberal digital culture. *Journal of Gender Studies, 27*(2), 231–241.

Henry, M. V., & Farvid, P. (2017). 'Always hot, always live': Computer-mediated sex work in the era of 'camming'. *Women's Studies Journal, 31*(2), 113–128.

Jones, A. (2015). For black models scroll down: Webcam modelling and the racialisation of erotic labour. *Sexuality and Culture, 19,* 776–799.

Jones, A. (2016). "I get paid to have orgasms": Adult webcam models negotiation of pleasure and danger. *Signs: Journal of Women in Culture and Society, 42*(11), 227–256.

Jonsson, L. S., & Svedin, M. H. (2014). 'Without the internet, I would never have sold sex: Young women selling sex online. *Cyberpsychology: Journal of Psychosocial Research on Cyberspace, 8*(1), 1–14.

Kaul, A., & Chaudhri, V. (2017). Do celebrities have it all? Context collapse and the networked publics. *Journal of Human Values, 24*(1), 1–10.

Khamis, S., Ang, L., & Welling, R. (2016). Self-branding, 'micro-celebrity' and the rise of social media influencers. *Celebrity Studies, 8*(2), 191–208.

Lane, F. (2000). *Obscene profits: The entrepreneurs of pornography in the cyber age.* London: Routledge.

Litt, E., & Hargittai, E. (2016). The imagined audience on social network sites. *Social Media and Society,* 1–12.

MacPhail, C., Scott, J., & Minichiello, V. (2015). Technology, normalisation and male sex work. *Culture, Health & Sexuality, 17*(4), 483–495.

Marwick, A. E. (2013). *Status update: Celebrity, publicity and branding in the social media age.* New Haven: Yale University Press.

Marwick, A. E., & Boyd, D. (2010). I Tweet honestly, I Tweet passionately: Twitter users, content collapse and the imagined audience. *New Media & Society, 13*(1), 114–133.

Mathews, P. W. (2017). Cam models, sex work and job immobility in the Philippines. *Feminist Economics, 23*(3), 160–183.

Mackinnon, C. A. (1987). Feminism unmodified. *Discourses on life and law.* Cambridge: Harvard University Press.

Paasonen, A. (2010). Labors of love: Netporn, web 2.0 and the meanings of amateurism. *New Media & Society, 12*(8), 1297–1312.

Page, R. (2012). The linguistics of self-branding and micro-celebrity in Twitter: The role of hashtags. *Discourse & Communication, 6*(2), 181–201.

Race, K. (2015). Speculative pragmatism and intimate relationships: Online hook ups devices in online life. *Culture, Health and Sexuality, 17*(4), 496–511.

Sanders, T., & Hardy, K. (2015). Students selling sex: Marketization, higher education and consumption. *British Journal of Education, 36*(5), 747–765.

Sanders, T., Scoular, J., Campbell, R., Pitcher, J., & Cunningham, S. (2018). *Internet sex work beyond the gaze.* London: Palgrave Macmillan.

Shah, N. (2007). PlayBlogs: Pornography, performance and cyberspace. In K. Jacobs, M. Janssen, & M. Pasquinelli (Eds.), *C'Lick me: A netporn studies reader* (pp. 31–44). Amsterdam: Institute of Network Cultures.

Van Doorn, N., & Velthuis, O. (2018). A good hustle: The moral economy of market competition in adult webcam modeling. *Journal of Cultural History, 11*(3), 177–192.

Walsh, M. J., & Baker, S. A. (2017). The selfie and the transformation of the public-private distinction. *Information, Communication & Society, 20*(8), 1185–1203.

Weiss, B. R. (2018). Patterns of interaction in webcam sex work: A comparative analysis of female and male broadcaster. *Deviant Behaviour, 39*(6), 732–746.

Wesch, M. (2009). YouTube and you: Experiences of self-awareness in the context of the collapse of the recording webcam. *Explorations in Media Ecology, 8,* 19–34.

6

Conclusion: The Governance of Male Sex Work in Digital Cultures

Abstract Ryan offers a brief conclusion highlighting the significance of greater social media use by male sex workers on the sex industry in general. It also examines some of the implications of this transformation on the governance of sex work in the fields of law, health and safety.

Keywords Governance · Sex work · Internet

This book set out to explore the greater visibility of male sex work within new social media and understand how sex workers navigate these digital cultures. It was motivated by a desire to reconcile this visibility with a public policy silence that seemed incongruous at a time of heightened debate about the future of prostitution policy during the years 2015–2017. Was the retreat by gay-identified male sex workers deeper within social media servicing the LGBTQ community a localised response to new forms of governance criminalising sex work clients in Ireland or part of a global trend of mainstreaming on new digital platforms? There are undoubtedly local factors. The domination of digital male sex work by South American migrants reflected the political economy of the state's migration policy which, when combined with the

© The Author(s) 2019
P. Ryan, *Male Sex Work in the Digital Age*,
https://doi.org/10.1007/978-3-030-11797-9_6

visa's work restrictions and the high cost of accommodation in Dublin created conditions that could, theoretically at least, foster entry into sex work. While the stories of the central protagonists were not born in Ireland, this book is a new chapter in the history of Irish sexuality. This new chapter tells us about the continuing evolution of the LGBTQ community in Ireland as it integrates newly arrived migrants and how they in turn transform the very fabric of that community—from its club scene, music and technology—to the transformation of desire, sex and intimacy. It provides us with an understanding of the challenges too, telling stories that cast light on casual racism and stigma, a housing crisis, recreational drug use and rising rates of HIV infection. It builds upon and extends previous work on male sex work when different challenges were being grappled in Ireland.

This is a book about desire. It is about how we communicate that desire to others. I do not mean sexual desire exclusively, although it has played a central role in understanding sex worker lives. The stories in the book tell of cultivating sexual desire through the display of bodies that endure punishing fitness regimes and the intake of nourishing foods delivered with militaristic precision throughout the day. While the stories tell of generating sexual desire, it is also the deployment of that body as an agent of consumption in travel, food, friendships and music that commodifies not just the body, but the person themselves. Social media provided the platforms to showcase these bodies to communicate one's taste through consumption and realise a profile and personality worthy of following. Social media would offer versatility in communicating these multidimensional elements of male sex work that would prove increasingly attractive over traditional escort sites, although success would hinge on the self-branding and interactive and promotional strategies the men brought to bear. The book set out to understand the parameters of this interaction and the new conventions which governed it, building on the analysis of digital male sex work beyond a focus on advertising. This analysis would focus on how income is generated by virtue of having a high profile social media presence, in direct face-to-face meetings but increasingly through broadcasting monetised content.

The stories told in this book problematise our understanding of sex work based on existing scholarly accounts, where a disproportionate energy has focused on entry and exit points to sex work. While I have outlined a political-economy context within Ireland that set in motion my interviewees' engagement with sex work, these men had long being the beneficiaries of physical and erotic capital in Venezuela and Brazil. The engagement in intimate relationships that yielded economic and social advantages continued when the men re-located to Ireland, blurring the boundaries between sex work as is commonly conceived as the exchange of cash, to more open-ended beneficial arrangements. While these arrangements have historic precedents, the emergence of new social media and the presumed intimacy with which they can create with followers has made these beneficial arrangements easier to conceive and sustain. I have argued in the book that sex work appears more as a resource which is drawn down by men at specific times, rather than understanding it as a career or identity. Similarly, there is no distinct *exit* from sex work, rather a commitment to remain open to what the future held in terms of challenges and opportunities.

The near domination of the digital sex work market by South American men can be partially explained through migration policy but that success was also related to the value of their physical and erotic capital within the sexual marketplace. This was intertwined with their racialisation, which bestowed a range of imagined sexual and emotional characteristics upon my interviewees, which they integrated into the outward construction of their digital selves. This process of racialisation, which was potentially advantageous for some, also acted as a straightjacket for others. With Brazilian workers featuring prominently on escort sites and across dating sites like Grindr, interviewees admitted to changing their advertised nationality to Portuguese, to offset what they perceived as a damaged and overexposed Brazilian 'brand'. Similarly, Venezuelan nationals admitted to placing [Not Brazilian] text on their social media bios for the same reason, revealing the complexity of possessing racialised identities that are simultaneously desired and the bearer of stigma.

The men I interviewed for this book lived their lives on social media. Each social media account—Grindr, Instagram, Tinder or Twitter—portrayed a slightly edited version for different audiences with different motivations. Those most successful in adapting social media for the purpose of generating income through face-to-face meetings or the broadcast of monetised content had already established profiles with significant followings. This success combined digitally mediated photos and using strategies most commonly associated with micro-celebrity. The development of in-app features on both Instagram and OnlyFans, like video uploads, polling and live streaming facilitated the creation of intimacy and knowing, important for the maintenance of self-branding that could secure monetised content. In-app links in Grindr connected followers to Instagram and OnlyFans, with each platform promising to unlock greater intimacy. Instagram and OnlyFans supported my interviewees' sex work ambiguity and enabled them to retain a flexible presentation of the digital self. Even on Grindr, renowned for enabling fast sexual encounters, sex work remains communicated through a new genre of emoji, to avoid the suspension of accounts for commercial advertising. This enabled my interviewees to retain multiple digital identities and resist sex work stigma which they felt would impede upon the realisation of their employment, education or relationship goals.

Achieving micro-celebrity status on social media also presented challenges. The lack of anonymity brought my interviewees face to face with followers who were disappointed or angered by recent or no interaction. It made them more vulnerable to the experience of having their photos and videos reproduced and used without their consent by people creating fake accounts. It presented challenges in maintaining a boundary between a public/private life when that very dichotomy became inverted as family public events became private and private intimate moments became public. Trading heavily on physical and erotic capital on social media left my interviewees open to coercion by those who sought to take advantage of their precarious position in the country. It also became an impediment in forming relationships with those who remained cautious about their sexual histories, drug use and HIV status and their motivations to enter into permanent relationships with Irish nationals.

This book raises some important issues as we continue to understand male sex worker lives. The stories told here reveal diverse experiences. Eighteen men arrived in Dublin, each with different resources available to them—financial, educational, peer support—and united by the ability to convert their physical and erotic capital into economic opportunities. The success with which each man capitalised on their social media profiles was uneven, demonstrated by my concentration on just three accounts to illustrate the process. These three accounts represented the early adaptors of technology, like Onlyfans, recently launched in 2016, which requires considerable promotion on social media to transfer and broadcast monetised content here. Apart from these accounts in the book, scholars have little knowledge to assess the impact of Onlyfans on the sex industry, but there is no doubt that more sex workers will be drawn to this platform. These different accounts of sex work require us, as a society to remain vigilant to diverse needs. The embedding of male sex work within dating apps like Grindr, while offering flexibility and a beneficial ambiguity to workers, will make it increasing difficult, for health promotion agencies, for example, to target specific groups within a context of increased drug use and rising rates HIV infections (MacPhail et al. 2015: 491). This is compounded by the greater individualisation within social media-based sex work where not only is there is a lack of peer support, there is active competition and some hostility between workers. Safer sex, HIV testing and the use of PREP were topics that my interviewees were the least comfortable talking with me about.

Similarly, this further movement of sex work into social media makes the Criminal Law (Sexual Offences) Act 2017, which criminalised the purchase of sex, almost impossible to enforce within the complexity of the intimate relationships recounted in this book. The regulation of sex work has traditionally targeted publicly visible street work, often motivated by nuisance complaints or brothels. Sanders et al. (2018: 122, 127) found little evidence of a coordinated police strategy to regulate Internet sex work in the UK. There is little to suggest this situation would be any different in Ireland. The surveillance of digital sex work was not just an issue for local authorities, however. A number of my interviewees advertised on Dublin.cracker.com, an affiliate of the US Backpage.com, which the FBI closed down in 2018. The signing of the Stop Enabling Sex Traffickers Act (SESTA) 2018 into law by President Trump erodes the 'safe harbor' rule, making website providers liable if third parties were found to be advertising prostitution, leading to the closure of well-known sites like Craigslist's personal ads. This has raised fears over the ability of sex workers to continue to work safely indoors. A series of attacks on Brazilian trans sex workers in Dublin in 2017 gave rise to fears of the impact the sex purchase ban may have on the safe negotiation of sex work.[1]

The lives of the men whose stories contribute to this book have continued to change. Migrant sex work lives are transient. Six men chose to stay in Ireland, undertaking further education and working, five moved abroad—to the US, Italy, Portugal and the UK and seven returned home to Brazil. Their social media profiles developed so carefully during their time in Ireland continue to document this next stage of their lives.

Note

1. https://www.irishtimes.com/news/crime-and-law/dramatic-rise-in-attacks-on-sex-workers-since-law-change-1.3208370. Accessed May 4, 2018.

References

MacPhail, C., Scott, J., & Minichiello, V. (2015). Technology, normalisation and male sex work. *Culture, Health and Sexuality, 17*(4), 483–495.

Sanders, T., Scoular, J., Campbell, R., Pitcher, J., & Cunningham, S. (2018). *Internet sex work: Beyond the gaze*. Cham: Palgrave.

Index

© The Editor(s) (if applicable) and The Author(s) 2019
P. Ryan, *Male Sex Work in the Digital Age*,
https://doi.org/10.1007/978-3-030-11797-9